Free:

From Legalism to Grace

Breaking Out of the

United Pentecostal Church

Jennifer Brewer

A giant, heart-felt thank you needs to go out to the following people:

Jereme, the love of my life, you are my rock and my sanity.
My kids (all three of you), I apologize for all the quiet days we've had to have.
My parents, if it weren't for you, well, I wouldn't be here!
My friends, I am a hot mess without you guys, your assistance and or encouragement has been priceless:
Kelly, Valencia, Jamie, Mike, Aaron, Hannah, Katie, Lisa
Also, all my work people, I am sorry for all of the book talk! Thank you for your patience with me!

Table of contents

Why

I have loved to write since I was a child and have wanted to write a book for as long as I can remember. The problem has always been, I had no idea what to write about. Then, sometimes, material presents itself. I procrastinated beginning because I am growing and learning more things about myself and God's grace every day so I was waiting until I had it all together to start. Then it dawned on me, I don't intend to stop growing and learning, plus, let's face it; I will never have it all together!

This book is my life, both literally and figuratively. As I am telling my story, it is healing my emotional wounds but also, hopefully, this book will make its way into the hands of someone else who needs to hear how much they are loved and wanted by their Creator. Maybe, just maybe someone, somewhere who has been questioning their current spiritual situation will read this and relate on some level. Perhaps, someone will read this, and find the inner strength and courage to make positive changes to better their emotional well being. Whatever the case, this book is about life and healing, while it is my personal story, I have no doubt; there will be many that will be able to relate.

For the first half of my life, I had no idea church hurt was real. I had no clue that people can experience panic attacks,

1

PTSD, and such serious debilitating triggers from spiritual trauma. I assumed such things were caused exclusively from far more "serious" life experiences like war. I wish I could go back to me fifteen years ago and clue that naïve little girl in. How much anguish would that have potentially saved me as well as my family? The thought is excruciating.

So, here it is; my journey out of the United Pentecostal Church organization. The church that claims they have the "whole gospel" and unique revelations given to them from God himself. The organization that has had its hold on way too many of my loved ones for far too long. The oppressive church organization that has such a way of presenting itself and its doctrines that even its ministers don't dare question the hierarchy of its leaders.

Here is how I overcame the fear of leaving, the fear of hell and the severe oppression I felt as a girl growing into a woman living out this religion's strict standards. This is my story of overcoming the feelings of inadequacy, and ugliness. My escape after many, many days of crying alone in the shower, feeling too depressed to even want to leave my home and feeling abandoned by God himself.

While this story is real, the names have been changed to protect the innocent. (That sounds so Law and Order!) But seriously, don't bother looking them up on Google or Facebook, you won't find them. I also think it is important to mention, I have no ill feelings toward anyone from my past or present. God has helped me make peace and bring forgiveness. So don't judge anyone that may be mentioned. They were probably just reacting in a way they thought was best, and my heart aches for them daily.

I want to crush the illusion that the only reason people leave the United Pentecostal Church organization is out of rebellion. I would love for those still in the religion to understand, the way they treat those who have left matters. Their words and actions affect people for lifetimes. But, I also want them to know I would love to walk side by side with them in this voyage of life, putting aside our differences and loving Jesus together.

Also, I must add, this is my perception of my time spent in the United Pentecostal Church organization, and may not always reflect the church's official stance on every topic.

I hope the main takeaway from this book is about discovering grace and healing, but to appreciate the ending, one must start from the beginning.

Chapter 1

The Beginning

I am standing in a room full of stick figures. I am not the same as them, I am a human, but I am trying my hardest from the middle of the pack to get their attention, I am screaming something, anything at the top of my lungs to get at least one of them to look toward me. But they don't, they are all standing facing me, but with their stick arms crossed over their stick torsos and noses up in the air, clearly ignoring my pleas for attention. I wake up from this nightmare crying and shaking in my mom's bed feeling like I was alone and forgotten. I was around seven years old the first time I dreamt of this. The feeling of emptiness the stick figures gave me became a reoccurring theme in my early years. It is the epitome of my childhood. I was always the outsider, always looking to fit in or get approval from my family and peers, but seemingly falling short every time.

While I am dreaming, my mom is in the other room having Bible study with a coworker. After me watching from a neighbor's window as my father placed half of our household furniture onto a moving truck and drove away, my mom was devastated and was trying desperately to build a new life with just her and me. She wanted God to be a big part of that new life. My mom was raised Baptist and after trying out a few churches in the area, we had started attending a large Baptist church with our neighbors. But my mom wanted more. She had tried and failed several times at religion and this time, she wanted it to stick.

She had met a man at the grocery store where she worked nights that had a recent divorce on his rap sheet as well and they bonded instantly. I imagine their meeting going something like this: she is working the front counter behind the register and he spots her from the dairy aisle, the angelic choir sings their song, his eyes lock with hers, and that was it! They were destined to live happily ever after! They didn't actually tell me this, but that is the version I am going with. He was United Pentecostal, or Apostolic as they commonly call themselves, (because they have the true doctrine of the Biblical apostles) and had offered to teach her a Bible Study, which he did, and then later became my stepdad.

To fully understand the significance of this religious transition, you need to know the basic beliefs of the United Pentecostal Church, (or UPC as we will call it from here on out). We will get into more details later, but the overview of their core doctrine is this:

The UPC teaches you will not be saved by the traditional belief in Jesus Christ alone as most other Christian denominations do. According to their doctrine, only those who have followed a three-step salvation plan based on Acts 2:38 will be saved.

Acts 2:38 in the King James Version reads:

Then Peter said unto them, Repent, and be baptized every one of you in the name of Jesus Christ for the remission of sins, and ye shall receive the gift of the Holy Ghost.

Step one is considered repentance, step two is baptism in Jesus' name, and step three is receiving the Holy Ghost. So, a conversion in a UPC church looks like this:

A "sinner" walks into the church, kneels at the altar and tells God they are sorry for their sins. Immediately, they are whisked away to be baptized, because if they were to die in a car accident on their way home, they still would not make it to heaven at this point. It is commonly taught that the act of baptism itself is what "washes away your sins", making the repentance part only a formality. Then, as soon as they come out of the water in the baptismal tank they have people laying hands on them trying to "pray them through" to receive the Holy Ghost. According to the UPC, someone has not received the Holy Ghost and has therefore not completed all of the steps of salvation, until they have spoken in tongues or a divine heavenly language (or oftentimes, some gibberish no one understands).

If you are converting from a more traditional Christian religion and had already been baptized in your last church, you most likely would have to get baptized again. Most denominations baptize according to Matthew 28:19. In this verse, Jesus says to baptize in the name of the Father, the Son, and the Holy Spirit, but the UPC vehemently denounces this form of baptism. This brings up the next major difference between the UPC and other churches; Trinity versus Oneness.

The UPC rejects the Trinity in their statement of faith and believes strictly Oneness. Meaning, they don't believe God is three divine persons. They believe the Father, Son, and Holy Spirit are interchangeable titles for Jesus Himself, not that each has their own place or roles in the Godhead.

6

Making baptizing in Jesus' name imperative, since baptism plays such a strong role in their salvation requirements.

So to break it down, without following the three specific steps means no eternal salvation. But it doesn't end there. In order for God to be pleased with you after you have completed the steps to salvation, you have to follow certain rules, such as women can never cut their hair, women can only wear modest skirts or dresses, men are discouraged or not allowed in certain churches to grow facial hair or wear shorts. The list drags on and on, and it can vary greatly from church to church. We will dive more into these "holiness standards" later on.

I realize to someone looking in, they would wonder why in the world anyone would get wrapped up in a religion so full of rules and regulations. Now, please keep in mind, this is before Google was a thing, and my mom was in a vulnerable place in her life, as are many who end up there. She fell for it all hook, line, and sinker.

We were snuggled in the recliner in the living room one evening and she got out her Bible. She told me we were going to switch churches. I was confused because we had friends at the large Baptist church but she explained it like this: "We want to attend a church that teaches the whole Bible. The church we are in now only teaches part." As she said this, she sectioned off a chunk of the pages. "Now don't you want to go to a church that teaches all the scriptures and not just some of them?" I thought about this for a while and agreed. Of course, I would rather learn the entire Bible, not just part! This is how the UPC grabs and keeps its members. Claiming they are a chosen people; they have been given the revelation of the "whole gospel".

We walked into our first UPC service when I was seven years old. It was a small church that was undergoing renovations at the time. There was only carpet in part of the sanctuary and tarps and tools everywhere. A woman greeted us at the door and led us to sit in her pew with her. Ironically, that woman ended up being my mother in law. I honestly don't remember too much of that first service, I was young, but my mom retells the story so well. She says her knees were shaking so hard and if it weren't for my mother in law sitting on the end of the pew, she would have run out. It was a typical UPC service, lots of singing, dancing, running the aisles, and speaking in tongues. The drums were loud and people were clapping and raising their hands. All of the women had big, fancy updos and everyone was dressed in their Sunday best. When the preacher spoke, it was not in a teaching tone, he would raise his voice very loudly while the congregation shouted "amen" and "hallelujah". It was very different from the reserved Baptist services we were used to.

After going for a few weeks, my mom and I were rebaptized the "correct" way, in Jesus' name, and my mom received the Holy Ghost on Halloween night in 1990. Looking in the mirror after service one evening shortly after, I told my mom, "I received the Holy Ghost too! Look at how I am smiling!" She quickly told me I hadn't, because I had yet to speak in tongues. I was devastated and vowed to myself to make sure I spoke in tongues so I could have the Holy Ghost as well. I was also terrified of hell, and wanted to fit in with the new friends I was making at the church, so I would try and try at the altar every service to speak in tongues. One night, with several people around me with their hands on my head, rocking me back and forth, they told me I did it, I had finally spoken in tongues. As a child, I took their word for it. To this day I honestly have no idea if I actually did or not, but at the time, I was ecstatic. I had completed the steps of salvation and was finally on my way to heaven! I was relieved. My mom was happy, and that made me happy.

Not long after my mother and I were baptized into this new church, she and my stepdad got married. Their love for each other was pure and simple so they opted for a wedding ceremony that immediately followed Sunday night church. My mom made me a beautiful, long flowery dress that I got to walk down the aisle in while holding peonies I had picked from our front yard. To a scraggly, awkward child, it was magical and I felt like a princess! I was excited to be gaining a new little brother in the transaction as well! Not to mention the other step-siblings I inherited who lived in a whole other state! I went from being the only child to gaining an entire family, it was a dream come true for me.

Chapter 2

Growing up Different

My biological father wasn't around often. I only went to his house when it was convenient for him. To be fair, my mom probably didn't make it very easy on him, but when I think about my relationship with my father, it pains me. I know if it were my children, I would have fought like hell to see them every chance I could. He didn't, and it hurt. He married my stepmom without me even knowing. One day, I went over to his house and found that he had moved to the neighboring state with her and her two children, this was how I found out I had gained two new siblings.

My stepmom is a wonderful person, but I am certain my mother put her through the wringer about religious differences. By the time she came into my life, I had begun abiding by all of the strict UPC rules. I was only wearing skirts and dresses and hadn't cut my hair since our conversion. My stepmom would do her best to help me dress for whatever the occasion by letting me wear my stepsister's swimsuit or snow pants, since I didn't own those items, and I would oblige as to not upset her. When I got home, however, I inevitably would tell on myself to my mother thinking I had committed some terrible sin by wearing snow pants to go sledding. I have no doubt my mother probably held that against my stepmom and told her so. I felt so torn, I wanted to do what was right and please God, but by going to my father's house, I always seemed to feel as if I had done something wrong. It was very confusing.

As if the life transitions I had already experienced by the age of eight weren't difficult enough for a child, after I finished the second grade, my mom decided public school was too worldly for me. So, for third grade, off to a private Christian school I went. By fourth grade, she determined even the Christian school wasn't appropriate, so she pulled me out of school altogether and began homeschooling me.

At first, I liked this idea. My family was really into a program at church called Bible Quizzing, which involves kids memorizing hundreds of Bible verses every year and then going to tournaments to compete over the material. This takes hours of studying a day and lots of repetition and discipline. It was convenient I didn't have to waste time going to school; I could focus all my time memorizing verses and practicing. With so much time to dedicate, I was becoming pretty good at it. I was not getting much attention from my biological father, so I longed to impress my stepdad by how well I could perform at these tournaments.

My days were primarily filled with reading books (exclusively Christian authors of course) and memorizing scriptures. Not much else to do when nearly everything else is considered worldly or evil. My parents had given up our television because the pastor told them to, so I couldn't even watch educational shows. I also remember asking to take ballet lessons, but that was nixed for several obvious reasons. After a short time of this life, I started to feel very

11

lonely during the weeks my stepbrother wasn't around. He was at our house every other week and I looked forward to him coming over to break up the monotony.

My family would go to Bible Quizzing tournaments one or two weekends a month for six months out of the year. Those trips doubled as our family vacations. My mom and stepdad were getting recognition in the Bible Quizzing circuit and people from around the state were beginning to know who they were. This became a bit of a problem for me as a young child, as my last name was different from the rest of my family. Just like in my stick figure dream, I was the outcast. People just assumed my last name was the same, so if they were to hear my full name, (which happened when they announced the highest scores of the tournament) they never knew who I was. That was crushing for a kid. I felt like my stepbrother fit into my family more than I did.

I remember one instance (it's weird the things your brain remembers) we were sitting at the kitchen table eating dinner and for whatever reason, the mayonnaise jar had a piece of masking tape on it right after the company's motto with my parent's last name. I'm sure they had brought the jar to a church potluck or something. My stepbrother picked up the jar that now read "Bring out the best"- and the piece of tape with the name that did not belong to me. We both were arguing about who was the best in the family when he astutely pointed out, I was not in fact the best, because that was not my name. I was crushed. He was right; I didn't fit in with my own family. I was still an outsider, even at home.

By the time I was in the fifth grade, I convinced my mom that I needed to be back in the public school. I was so very lonely at home without any friends and I had been to several church camps by this point where they encouraged us to bring our friends to church. I remember pointing out the fact to her, that if I only knew church friends, how can I invite anyone to church? Miraculously, she agreed and sent me

12

back to school under the condition she drove me and I did not ride the bus. In my mother's head, only terrible things happen on a school bus.

There was the problem of a co-ed gym class, however. Whatever would I wear that would be appropriate? It's difficult and immodest to wear a skirt for gym. I have learned to laugh at my mortification throughout the years and this is the perfect example. My mom, God love her, with all the purest, best intentions decided the proper thing to do for this situation would be to hand make me some culotte jumpers. Even in the 1990s, those were not cool. In case you are sheltered enough to not know what these are, culottes are ridiculously baggy pants that are made to look like a skirt. She made two, one for each gym day a week. So every Tuesday and Thursday I sported either a baby pink, calf-length jumper with clear buttons down the front, or a baby blue one with little flowers all over it. I still think about the fact that our class's D.A.R.E. day was on a gym day and laugh because that police officer, who often let me help him carry his things to his car, probably thought those hideous jumpers were the only pieces of clothing I owned!

And then, there was the line dancing segment of public school PE. Dancing of any sort is considered worldly by the UPC unless you are "in the Spirit" dancing at a church service. In that case, for some reason, it is perfectly acceptable. I sat in the corner of the elementary school gym with a note from my pastor explaining dancing was prohibited for his congregants. I watched the rest of my classmates dosey doe and spin around allowing myself to feel self-righteous because that was the better alternative than feeling sad for being left out once again. Moments like these are when little seeds of arrogance and pride start to creep in. As a child, I felt as if I was better than the rest of my classmates, who were participating in such a worldly activity such as dancing. God had chosen me above them to

13

reveal that such behavior was a sin. It is easier to squash the loneliness when you approach things from this perspective.

One time during gym class, while sporting those super cool culottes, our class was outside playing softball and a boy decided it would be a good idea to spit on me. I didn't know what to do, so I just stood there frozen and took it. I came home that evening and told my mom, who was fit to be tied. I told her, not to be mad because Jesus was spit on too. To this day, I still don't know if that was a good attitude to have or a very warped one. I was teased mercilessly at school, it killed what little self-esteem I had, but I took it in stride. This was for the greater cause, and I was being a witness for God through my ridicule. But kids were cruel, we had no money for name brand shoes or clothes and my stringy hair, buck teeth, and giant glasses didn't help matters any. I tried to fit in, but kids are kids, acceptance was ultimately unattainable.

By the end of elementary school, my visits with my father became more and more sporadic. I was so torn. I wanted a relationship with him, but I also wanted so badly to fit in with my mom and stepdad, but without their last name it seemed impossible. However, my father was worldly and drank beer; so clearly, I wasn't a part of his family either. I felt as I was a piece of paper just blowing by itself through the wind. I took my feelings out on my stepbrother a lot. I was pretty mean to him. Although, honestly, I had never had a sibling before and I just thought that's what siblings did. But, he took a lot of my hurt in the form of wedgies, and verbal confrontations. I do feel bad now. Okay, maybe not for the wedgies, he probably deserved those! But for all of the straight-up mean things I said to him through the years, he didn't deserve that.

I feel like at this point of your reading, you may be thinking my life was a giant tragic mess. It really wasn't. Without a doubt, at my mom's house, we were the Focus on

14

the Family family. We had weekly game nights and devotions. Dinner was always homemade and served at the table. My mom handmade a lot of my clothes and typed the church bulletin on an old typewriter. We even had songbooks in the car so we could sing hymns as a family on the way to church! These things just became the norm for me, and I didn't realize other people didn't do them. A lot of my friends from the church would come over to our house to hang out there. My parents were always welcoming to anyone who wanted to come and have dinner with us. My best friend from church, Marie, was at our house constantly. She and I would make hand made scrunchies for our hair and practice the crazy UPC hairstyles on each other to pass the time.

Marie and I got into a lot of trouble together as kids. We were so mean! We would put tacks in the other girl's chairs during Sunday School and passed notes to each other in Bibles during church service. Our pastor would often stop in the middle of his sermon to reprimand us. "Girls!" he would say looking up at us over his reading glasses. One time, I accidentally flipped a button from my sweater over the pew in front of me during the middle of his sermon. He thought it was a piece of candy, so he stopped preaching and told me to pick it up, then after service, he promptly escorted Marie and me to his office to scold us for eating candy during church.

My mom and stepdad were sincere Christians inside and out and gave selflessly of their time and finances to the church until there was literally nothing left to give. This caused them to be very frugal with their money. Yet, as stressful as that had to have been, they seemed to conquer life with grace and humor and gave me many memories of them laughing at whatever circumstance they found themselves in.

One time, in particular, we were headed home from a relative's house from out of state and the alternator was going out in the little Ford Escort we were driving. Naturally, as these things go, it was night time and raining. I remember my mom hanging out the window wiping the rain off with napkins so my stepdad could continue to drive without wipers or headlights. They laughed and laughed about this. That is just how they were. Always counting their blessings letting everything else just breeze right off their shoulders. Now that I am an adult, I tend to respond to things in the same manner, my husband, not so much. I think my laughter at his frustration sometimes makes him wonder why he married me!

By the time I was twelve, I decided I didn't want to have a relationship with my biological father any longer. He had stood me up on multiple visitation occasions and I was overwhelmed with the insecurity of never fitting in. In my twelve-year-old brain, I thought if I could be done with the home where I had no chance to fit in, my stepdad could adopt me and I would finally officially be a part of a family because my name would be the same as theirs, making my life easier.

I think a lot of this feeling stemmed from the church. I wanted my name to portray that I was indeed who they thought I was; my parent's child from a perfectly religious, Bible Quizzing home. I told my mother this, who was overjoyed at the prospect of never having to deal with my father again. She asked him to terminate his rights.

The way it seemed to me as a child, this was when my father decided he gave a crap about me, or maybe he felt it was the perfect opportunity to screw me over one more time. I really don't know. I'd like to think now that he was just doing the best he could, and didn't know what else to do. I think that is the story that I am going to go with. Whatever the case, his actions scarred me.

He told my mom that he would terminate his rights and allow my stepdad to adopt me if I called and told him myself that is indeed what I wanted. I was twelve. I hated the idea of hurting him, but my hurt was bigger. So I did it. I called and told him I no longer wanted to see him and to please terminate his rights. I cried and cried through every moment of that conversation. It was terrible. He never followed through. I hated him for it. So I just kept on pretending he wasn't my father and tried and tried to mentally include myself in what I thought was my perfect Christian home.

My dream of stick figures continued throughout elementary and thanks to a very realistic play put on by my church, I also started having nightmares about hell and missing the rapture. The play was about a teenager who had committed various sins such as looking at pornography and going to parties. In one big final hurrah, the teen went to a party and got into a drunken car accident. Demons promptly escorted him straight to hell; all the while the devil (emphasized with a strobe light and terrifying demonic laughter) was pounding nails into the teenager's coffin so he could not be raised in the rapture, the event when Jesus comes back for those who are sinless. I must say, it put the fear of God in me and I was scared to death of getting left behind when Jesus came back and Satan dragging me off to hell.

Waking in the morning covered in sweat and my heart racing became the norm for me. I would often have very vivid recurring dreams. In one of my recurring dreams, I would be standing in the kitchen of the church, washing dishes with my friend. She was the rebellious one, and I was always the goody-two-shoes going the extra mile for Jesus. We are splashing in the water and laughing, and we hear the trumpet blow indicating the rapture was happening. I immediately look at her, fearing she didn't make the cut but thinking surely I would, I am the one who did everything

17

right. I only made it as high as the ceiling. After several minutes of watching everyone else around us fly up to the sky, she and I look at each other in sheer terror. We didn't make it. We got left behind. I didn't understand, she was the bad one and I was good, why didn't I make it to heaven with all the rest of the church? I didn't sin like the boy in the drama did, what did I do wrong? This idea haunted me daily. If my mom was ever late to pick me up from school, I was in an instant panic. Did the rapture happen? Was I left behind and headed to hell?

I entered middle school as awkwardly as expected. By this age, thankfully, my mom allowed me to exchange my giant wire-framed glasses for contact lenses and I got braces for my ridiculous overbite. Things were starting to look up.

I did get asked a lot in middle school if I was Amish. Now, I understand why a child would think I was, I did wear a skirt every day. Back then, however, it was super annoying to me. My comeback line was always, "Um, no, my family owns a car!" How original! I still felt like the school was my mission field, so I tried to not let things get to me.

Finding people to sit with in the cafeteria at lunch became a bit of a challenge. I actually had one girl threaten to stab me if I sat by her. I never did sit completely by myself, but I was always the one squeezing in on the end and never talking to those around me. I pretty much just walked the hallways with my head down and kept to myself.

While the middle school experience itself was pretty dark and lonely for me, on the church front, this age was an exciting time. In the UPC, when you turn twelve, you get to join the youth group. I waited impatiently for my 12th birthday because Marie is nine months older than me and had already gotten to "move up". She always seemed to get to do everything before I did! She wore a bra before me, her mom let her wear pantyhose before my mother allowed me, she had a boyfriend before I did, everything! And clearly, she

18

never missed the opportunity to throw that fact in my face. (Now, since we are pushing the big 40, I never let her forget she is the older one!) Once we started going to youth events like camp and Youth Convention, we were inseparable and she would stay long stretches at a time at my house. We both came from divorce ridden homes and bonded over that fact. We would cry together at the altar during youth functions and lean on each other for support when our parents disappointed us yet again. Even though I had little to no communication with my father during this time, the scars still remained.

Middle school was also when I started going with my husband, Jereme! How crazy messed up is that? I don't regret marrying him for a second; he is the most amazing person I have ever met, but middle school? Yikes, I was way too young for that mess! But when you are a lonely, awkward teenager, if someone finds you attractive and shows you affection in any way, you are drawn to them like a moth to a flame. He was just as awkward though, so I suppose it was fitting we were together. (Sorry honey)

Obviously, my mom was not a fan of me hanging out with any boys, especially a boy whom I claimed as my boyfriend. By the time I was in eighth grade, I was hanging out with Jereme and his best friend (both of whom had cars) almost exclusively. My mom was petrified of us having premarital sex and banned all physical contact. One time, during a Bible Quizzing tournament trip, my mom caught his arm around me in the back of the church van and she blew a gasket! As a parent of teenagers now, I understand where she was coming from, however, back then I resented her for her old fashioned rules. Because she was so strict, Jereme and I became professionals at sneaking around, and I had already made it to third base before I was in high school.

By the end of my middle school career, being at school was nothing but lonely for me. I still wanted to be a good

19

witness and bring people to my church, but it became harder and harder to put up with the bullying. Then, in eighth grade, God gave me Shelby. She was new to the school and was assigned to be my locker partner. She was a Christian from a strong, healthy religious family. She was a dancer and had an absolutely electric personality. Shelby included me in her tribe and I was incredibly grateful. I envied the fact she immediately had so many friends, but at the same time, I pitied her because even though she claimed to be a Christian, she attended one of those "easy believism" churches I had been warned about and despite all her goodness was bound for hell. This meant, she believed salvation came upon simply believing in Jesus, not three separate steps that included speaking in tongues. This bothered me. We became pretty close, (as close as my mom would allow me to be to someone who wasn't of our faith) and I saw how sincere her family was. It made me sad to think such a good family wouldn't get to go to heaven. It didn't seem fair. So every opportunity I could find, I would invite her to my church in hopes she would see the error of her ways and convert. I feel so guilty now when I look back at how arrogant I was to think for a second I was better than her in any way just because of my religion. Thankfully, I don't think she ever picked up on my hidden agenda, and I have since apologized to her.

The summer between middle school and high school, I was feeling guilty about my relationship with my biological father. It had been two years since we had spoken so I decided to call him on Father's Day to try and mend the hurt I thought I created by asking him to terminate his rights. His words to me during that phone conversation were that I had missed his birthday in May. I was crushed and hung up the phone feeling even worse than before I had called. The emotions of insecurity and abandonment flooded back and once again and I vowed to never speak to him.

When I started high school, I was just ready to be finished with school. I was done with the religious questions and the hierarchy of the cliques. I had Shelby and a few other friends who accepted the weirdo in the skirt, but overall, my social life was mostly at church. At church, I was the popular one; I was the in-crowd. My parents were pretty well known around the UPC for Bible Quizzing in our state by this point and up until I started rebelling when I was around sixteen, I was pretty good at the quizzing thing myself. Since we traveled frequently for quizzing and church functions, I was around other UPC teenagers a lot. While Jereme and I still dated on and off, Marie and I never missed an opportunity to flirt with the boys and come home with phone numbers. I will never forget after one such trip, I had given my home phone number to a boy from out of state. This was before cell phones were a thing and he called our home landline at 7 A.M. on Christmas! My mom was so mad! I thought it was hilarious.

Being a teenager in the UPC you attend yearly Youth Conventions and summer camps. At these meetings were hundreds and sometimes thousands of other UPC young people. I always looked forward to these trips because it was nice to be surrounded in a bubble of other young people like myself for a few days.

The schedule for such conventions would include two to three church services daily with shopping or other activities in between. As a girl, you didn't have too much free time between services because you would be busy getting ready for night service by dressing in your finest clothes (usually a modified prom dress) and the highest heeled shoes you could find. No convention outfit would be complete without spending hours on your long hair, curling and teasing it to new heights. I have heard it said by UPC women, "The higher your hair, the closer you are to Jesus!" Some of the hairstyles I sported back then, there really are no words to describe them!

During these church services, you would hear messages with pretty much the same theme every year. On the first day or two, you would be told about how you are a sinner. The ministers tend to hyper-focus on things such as sliding on the standards (trimming your hair or sneaking out of the house in pants), not praying enough, witnessing enough, or supporting your pastor enough. The idea always seemed to be you were never good enough on your own and needed to obey and submit to your pastor. He knows what is best for you. The minister would have an altar call at the end of the service and people would gather around the front, weeping, crying and speaking in tongues loudly for an hour or more. They never seemed to give any practical, real-life direction or advice to help you obtain the goals of perfection, just hammered in the fact, you are a sinner. No message of the cross, or redemption, just condemnation. Most of these services I left feeling worse than when I came.

By the last night of the convention, the minister usually didn't get a chance to actually speak. It was always a given the last night was the "shout down" service. This night was usually hours of loud music with people dancing around and shouting. At this service, the minister would generally take the microphone and start shouting things about how you should feel blessed because you are a "chosen generation, a peculiar people" (1 Peter 2:9). You have been given the exclusive "revelation of Jesus name" or the "whole truth" over every other denomination. God chose you above everyone else in all the other churches to experience such a "move of God". A lot of bashing other religious denominations tends to go on.

The feeling I always seemed to have by the time I experienced the last service of the conference was arrogance. I walked with my back a little straighter, my head held higher because God chose me specifically over all the other poor people in the world who attended those other types of churches. "Many are called, but few are chosen" (Matthew 22:14). This verse and many like it are used to make you feel special about being in the UPC. If you were uncomfortable at school looking different, you shouldn't. You should feel proud of your attire because that was your heritage. But, no real life change or heart change ever happened for me.

As I grew older, because I was learning I was better than others, I started unintentionally judging people based on their clothing, not on their actions, and I looked down on those who looked different than me. It started showing big time in the way I handled religious questions at school. I learned to deflect and just answer rudely, "It's my religion" when asked why I wore a skirt every day. I depended solely on my attire to be my witness for Christ and not my actions or attitude towards others. A harsh reality for people who grow up in a religious system based on works.

By the time I was sixteen, Marie was pretty much my only close friend who knew all of my secrets. She knew the details of the situation with my father and how I carried so much guilt for not wanting to have a relationship with him. I thought if I was supposed to be bringing him to Christ, I should be the one to make amends. Looking back now that is such a big responsibility to have been laid upon a child's shoulders.

So one day out of the blue, Marie and I were driving home from a 6 Flags trip in my rust bucket Nissan Sentra, a five-speed, with no air conditioning or radio discussing our parents. It was the dead of summer, we probably smelled so bad! I decided to swing by my father's house just to see if I still remembered where he lived. I did, and Marie convinced me to knock on the door. My stepmom answered and was so excited to see us, she started to tear up. I think she always wanted my father and me to have a relationship, but just didn't understand my hang-ups. We actually had a decent visit. I was pleasantly surprised at the welcome we received. This was the turning point for us. Not that we were instantly close after this encounter, but it was the beginning of at least us attempting to talk to each other.

After leaving my father's house I told my mom where I had been. She was not as thrilled as I had been about our visit. I think she felt, it would be too hard on me to try and cultivate my relationship with my father, and as an adult, now, I completely understand her hesitation given our history. She didn't ever stop me from speaking to him, however, and I respect her for that.

Chapter 3

Adulting in the UPC

Two months after my seventeenth birthday, Jereme proposed. I was ecstatic! We ate dinner at the fanciest restaurant I had ever been in and rode a carriage ride around town. My ring was small, but I thought it was beautiful! A little heart-shaped solitaire on a gold band, I felt so grown up wearing it. My relationship with my mom was starting to become a bit rocky as I was more and more disengaged with our eccentric Christian home life, and her strict rules. I felt like marriage was my ticket out. Having a daughter this age now, it seems so cringy to me to think about her even contemplating marriage at such a young age, but as a teenager, I thought I had life all figured out. Jereme and I were having sex regularly at this point, which was a huge sin and I had so much guilt and shame; I just wanted to be married so I wouldn't go to hell.

Wedding planning began my junior year of high school and by the time I was a senior, I had accumulated enough credits to attend school for only two hours a day for one semester. I graduated at the end of the first semester, missing my senior prom and my graduation ceremony. We were married two months later.

It poured down rain the entire day of our wedding. I have heard if it rains on your wedding day that you will have good luck. It must be true since we are still together! My father attended my wedding, but my stepdad was the one who walked me down the aisle. I am sure that it was hard for my father to watch, but I appreciated him showing his support for me by just being there. It meant a lot to me then, but as I have gotten older, I have come to realize how humbling it probably was for him. I am grateful he stuck it out.

Oh, how stupid and immature we were back then! As young newlyweds, we had zero money, but we thought we did! Jereme had bought a zippy little bright red Dodge Neon right before we got married and we rented a hole of an apartment on the top floor of an old house. Our close friends were living in the space right below us and we all thought we were living the high life! This apartment was so bad, the one clothes closet was in the kitchen and the bathroom was across the hallway. And I don't mean across the hall from our bedroom. I mean, we literally had to leave our unit and walk across the hallway to the bathroom. We had a bathroom key that hung on the wall on a hook by the front door!

We drove halfway across the country in that little Neon for our honeymoon. We were so poor, we ate nothing but peanut butter sandwiches on the way there and back and stayed with my grandparents for a night to save money. We had the best time! That was also when I tried alcohol for the first time. Nobody cards you in a honeymoon suite at an all-inclusive resort! We thought we were so grown up ordering Pina Coladas and champagne!

After we returned home from our honeymoon, Jereme and I bought a television and a DVD player. It was so exciting for me because it was a twenty-five-inch screen and I could watch whatever movies I wanted! At home, my parents had finally caved a few years prior and bought an old fifteen-inch computer monitor that my brother had hooked a Playstation into. We also realized a video camera we owned would double as a VCR so we watched a lot of Little Mermaid and George of the Jungle! Those were pretty much the only movies deemed appropriate enough for us to watch. It's so funny to think about now how a monitor and a video camera were acceptable to watch movies on, but a television and actual VCR were taboo! Jereme and I also started going to the theater, another thing that is forbidden by the stricter churches in the UPC. I had only been a few times after we had converted. Once, my stepdad snuck me out and had me swear to secrecy to not tell my mom he had taken me to see Titanic. The other movie I had seen before I got married was an R rated movie my older stepbrother took me to. Needless to say, I learned quite a few things by watching that movie!

As a young married couple, we did have several discussions concerning the church, but I don't remember if we had ever contemplated leaving at this point. I honestly don't know if the thought even occurred to us as an option. We did, however, agree that we did not believe in some of the standards the organization upheld such as women's clothing, no television or theaters and no jewelry. We vowed to never raise our kids believing such things, but to teach them to live them out anyway as we did, simply out of submission to our pastor. We thought the UPC had salvation correct, and we didn't want to hurt our families by not looking the part, so we just lived it. When that is all you know, it really isn't too hard to comply even when you don't agree. The fear of hell is bigger than any doubts anyway, and the UPC portrays your inconveniences as from a martyr standpoint, so your feelings seem irrelevant.

Six months after we got married, we bought our first home. It was a cute, little two-bedroom house in the middle of a small town not all too different than Mayberry from the Andy Griffith show. I am a little proud of us for accomplishing homeownership at such a young age. I was only eighteen and Jereme was twenty-one.

Not too long after we bought our house, 911 happened. I was at work at the time, and the young, sheltered me didn't even know what the World Trade Center was. When Jereme and I got home from work, we decided we would hook our television up to the antenna that the previous owners had left on the roof of the house. This was the first time since I was a small child I had a working TV in my house.

I remember watching the news for hours on end horrified at the images of those poor people jumping from the burning buildings. I had never seen anything like it. My generation in America had never seen anything like it. I am thankful I had the opportunity not to witness the horrific act of violence, but witness my country putting aside religious differences for that short time and come together as one. What would make this experience so crazy to most people is the fact that even then, after hooking up our TV just to watch such a historical event unfold, we still felt like we had to justify our actions to our parents by saying we planned on unhooking the antenna after the aftermath of 911 was over. Of course, we didn't. We enjoyed the freedom of being able to come home from work and relax on the couch together with our giant Rottweiler, Princess and watch a television show. After a few months, we called the cable company and had them install a box so we could get more channels! We really have always been a little rebellious.

Six months after we moved into our tiny house, I got pregnant. It seemed like the natural progression of things. You get married, buy a house and have a kid. Honestly, the pregnancy was a little bit of a shock because in my head I

28

thought birth control would take months to get out of my system, making me twenty years old before I had a baby. That is indeed not the truth, I conceived immediately. I was two months shy of my twentieth birthday when I had my daughter Jocelynn.

She was such a tiny, beautiful little thing. She looked perfect, like a porcelain doll. Born five weeks premature, she came home after a stint in the neonatal ICU with an IV port in her head for medication. I remember being scared to death I was going to break her somehow because let's be honest, I had no idea what I was doing with a baby, especially a baby so small! Miraculously, she is still with us, so I guess I didn't screw up too badly! To this day, I still can't believe they allowed such inexperienced parents to walk out of a hospital with a tiny human!

I loved being a mom! Jocelynn was such a good baby, she made it easy. We took her everywhere and she was just as content as could be. She was very social and people seemed to gravitate to her wherever she was. She is still like that, I'm not sure where she got her personality because it was not from her father, and it definitely wasn't from her mom who, most days, would rather hide under a chair than talk to people.

By the time Jocelynn was two, we were having some difficulties in the church Jereme and I had grown up in. One family, in particular, was making things especially hard on my parents. One Sunday morning, I walked in on my step-dad crying in a back room. When I asked him what was wrong, he told me he had overheard people saying ignorant things about him from the other room. I assume they didn't know he was within earshot of their pettiness. I thought (and still do) that my stepdad was the kindest and most sensitive person alive and the fact someone could speak ill of him made me absolutely livid. That was the last Sunday we were there.

29

Jereme and I talked about taking a church break for a while. We were continuing to question the belief system we had been taught since childhood and weren't completely sure what we believed. We had just suffered a miscarriage and were a little shaken and emotional from that experience the thought of searching for a new church seemed daunting. We never did tell either of our families about our doubts. My family left that church as well, the same Sunday and shortly after we had a family meeting. We decided, as a family, we would try out three other United Pentecostal churches in the area for a month each to see if we liked, or felt called to any of them. We decided to do this together as a family and see where it led. Jereme and I went along.

The first church we tried was small, a congregation of maybe fifty people. It was a branch off of the church we had just left, and there were a lot of similarities. The second church we visited was the church our previous pastor told us to stay away from. I have no idea why he was so adamant we didn't attend there, I assume it was a combination of anger because a lot of his flock had already started going there and grievances from past interactions with the pastor. We instantly fell in love with this church, however, and decided to stay. We knew many of the people already, so it made the transition easy.

It seems so unreal looking back at the struggle of finding a new church, but you have to understand, in the UPC, if you switch churches within the same geographical area, you are considered by many to be a church hopper. Many people from your former congregation will take your leaving very personally and will no longer view you as a close friend. You potentially lose or alter many of your lifelong friendships. The pastor at our new church made the transition as easy as possible though. We didn't feel like the pastors were as pretentious as the previous church we attended and we liked the apparent authenticity of the leadership. And of course, the love-bombing we received, helped as well.

Things about the pastor and his wife impressed me at first glance; things such as seeing him vacuum the fellowship hall after a church dinner, or the way his wife was warm and open to talk to you about her insecurities. They seemed so down to earth. I appreciated these small things after leaving a church where the pastor didn't even eat meals with the mere saints. We quickly became close friends with the pastors whom we will call, Rob and Barb. They doted on Jocelynn and having a daughter close to the same age themselves, it seemed like a perfect friendship.

My parents swiftly became involved with the children's ministry picking up right where they left off from the last church. They started a Bible Quizzing program and we had Jocelynn begin quizzing at the age of three. My step-brother became involved in youth activities and I began participating in the music. Things started to settle down and normalize on the church front.

Jereme and I had been trying to find a new home during this time and finally decided on a small subdivision that was building modest homes in our price range. We told another couple we had a history with who attended our new church and they happened to be looking into building a house as well. Whether it was by coincidence or God I have no idea, but somehow, through a serious of circumstances, we ended up with lots next door to each other. We thought it was great having another UPC family live near us. When you look the part of religious zealots, it's comforting to know people who are on your side are so close.

Jocelynn turned three the month we moved into our new house. We had a birthday party/house warming party at the same time the week after we moved in! What possessed me to think that was a good idea I will never know! We had been attending our church for eleven months at this point, and had many of our new friends over to celebrate. It was great fun with a piñata, cake, and games. Life appeared to be falling into place, on the outside.

Behind closed doors, there was sadness, loneliness, and depression. I hated who I was, both inside and out. I felt like there was something terribly wrong with me. I wasn't happy like I was supposed to be. I had everything, a husband who loved me, a beautiful daughter, a new home, a good job, and a church that preached "the truth" but I still felt empty. My marriage suffered. Jereme and I became more like roommates than life partners. We didn't fight often, but just kind of inhabited the same space. Something just seemed like it was missing. I often cried in the shower when no one could see. I felt dead inside. I tried to pray when I went to church, but it seemed like I didn't fit in there either. I am not an emotional, demonstrative person, and in a UPC service, those traits feel like a prerequisite to effective prayer.

The UPC has a term they use called "praying through". This means praying until you are bawling your eyes out, speaking in tongues. Some people take it a level further and jump or dance, shout loudly or even lay on the floor. I've heard people howling and squealing, seen people jump from pews or the platform, or run around the church, this is just not me. In all my years of being Pentecostal, I was never able to bring myself to do such things. I thought I had a spiritual problem, which added to my emotional distress. I felt like I was slowly being suffocated. I tried to do the things I was told would make me "grow spiritually". I would go through spurts of making sure I read my Bible for so long and listen only to church music, but it never seemed to stick or to make anything better.

To add to the spiritual distress, when you dress over the top modestly, only wearing certain types of clothing and have limited ways to fix your hair, you feel ugly. You feel ugly all the time. There are no other ways to sugar coat it, I

32

felt ugly. So when a man from my office started making advances towards me, I was flattered. My marriage was dull and I hadn't felt a romantic spark in a while, hence I was very receptive to the attention. This is hard to write and even harder to admit, but I seriously thought about leaving. The thought haunted me continually, and honestly, I probably would have gone through with it, if it hadn't been for my daughter. Having grown up in a divorced parents situation myself, I refused to do that to her. So I decided to quit my job to avoid temptation and I focused all of my energy on Jocelynn.

Not long after I became a stay at home parent, Jereme and I attended a church marriage retreat out of town. This was the weekend that saved my marriage. I think both of us realized changes needed to be made to preserve our relationship and we were committed to working on them. Having gotten married so young, we basically grew up together, and in the growing up process, we had become two different people. Divorce, however, was not an option and we were determined to fix us. I realized how important physical connection is to men and even though I did not feel attractive, I began trying to put his needs first. He learned things like communication and dishes were important to me, and he made an effort to make that a priority. Slowly but surely, we became closer until the idea of me leaving wasn't even in the back of my mind.

That same summer, I found out I was pregnant. Having experienced miscarriages in the past, Jereme and I were reluctant to tell anyone in the beginning. Once we reached a point we felt it was safe, we told our church "family". Our pastor was a little irritated with us because we had waited so long to tell them. He made a compelling point by saying they were our family and if something had gone wrong, they would want to be there to support us. I feel like he meant it and had good intentions, and I was appreciative. This is where the emotional part of the organization is tricky. While you are in, you are closer than friends, you are a family. The us versus the rest of the world mentality naturally happens because that is how you tend to view things from the inside.

Another thing that happened this summer stuck with me. My father had bought a house on a lake and in an effort to spend some time with Jocelynn and I had invited us to stay with him for a few days just the three of us. I think he wanted to try and mend our relationship hurts and hang-ups. I was grateful and went along. He said something one day while we were sitting out on the dock I will never forget. "Are you happy? You never seem happy, and I never see you smile." That statement took me back a little. Of course, I was happy! Wasn't I? I proceeded to tell him how happy I was. I was saved and on my way to heaven. How blessed and happy was I? I am not sure if I convinced him, but I had managed to convince myself. At least at that moment, I was convinced. At that very moment, I felt better than him and appalled that someone who wasn't saved could even question my life choices. But that small observation from a non-Apostolic replayed over and over again in my mind. Especially the days I stood in the shower with tears mixing themselves with the flowing water. Especially those days.

My pregnancy this time around went smoothly with no hiccups and we welcomed our son Jordin into the world surrounded by friends and family. My mother in law and Jereme's younger sisters traveled in for the occasion and with our pastor and his wife, all of my parents, our neighbors, and many other friends we constantly had a hospital room full of love and support. Once again, life seemed perfect on the outside.

Almost immediately life with Jordin became a challenge. He was not a happy, social baby like his sister, and was colicky a lot. He wasn't too fond of hugs and snuggles and once he started growing older, things such as shapes,

34

alphabet, and colors seemed to be difficult for him to grasp. He didn't play with his toys like a typical toddler. Instead, he would line them up and sort them into various groups. When he was old enough to be in a toddler bed, if there was anything at all on his floor and he noticed it, even in the middle of the night, he would come to get me crying about the "mess". Once his temper tantrums became uncontrollable, we reluctantly sought help from a psychiatrist. This is where our pastor Rob was incredibly helpful. Being a counselor himself, he advised us to seek professional help, not all UPC people feel this way, and I am thankful he advised us to do so. Mine and Jereme's parents weren't exactly on board at the beginning of this process. They tended to side more with the older, traditional UPC generation and thought the problem could be resolved through more disciplined parenting and prayer. And believe me, we had tried those things.

Jordin's fits were so intense it affected all of us. By the time he would finish crying, banging his head on the floor, breaking toys, hitting, kicking and biting for hours on end, everyone in the house would be in tears. It was awful. As a mother, I felt so helpless. Jereme and I felt like we had no choice but to get him professional help. After years of therapy sessions and tests (the mental health system in this country is broken, but that is another subject matter entirely) it was finally determined Jordin had level one autism with ADHD and anxiety. I remember sitting in that doctor's office holding back tears as the psychologist explained to me that Jordin is high functioning and would be able to do most jobs as an adult, but things would not always come easy for him, especially on the social front. He would probably be on medications for the rest of his life to control his anxiety and depression. I left heartbroken. I knew deep down something was not right, but to hear a professional say those things about your child from across a desk is difficult to take.

I felt I had failed as a parent. I know his diagnosis has nothing to do with my parenting skills, but at that moment, I still felt responsible in some way.

Getting medications worked out for Jordin was a life changer. Once we figured out the best plan for him, between therapy, medication and some parenting style changes he began to have fewer tantrums and his developmental delays caught up to normal range. The grandparents began to see maybe the medication was okay and even though the opinion of my parents ultimately did not change the way we approached this situation, it is always nice to have your parent's support, even when you are an adult.

During the process of determining Jordin's mental health diagnosis, it was also discovered he possessed a rare genetic disorder called MODY, or Mature Onset Diabetes of the Youth. Meaning, we were also dealing with elevated blood sugar levels as well as autism. There were times I felt like I was drowning. I was trying to focus my attention on Jordin, while also giving Jocelynn the mom she needed. Looking back now, I think she may have felt a bit passed over or forgotten during this time, as it lasted for years and took much of my energy. I pray she does not feel this way, I genuinely tried.

While we were going through all of Jordin's situations, the support we received from our close church "family" was amazing. We became even closer with Rob and Barb as they were a tremendous support system for us. I sang in an ensemble group at the church and those people became family to us. My neighbor was in this group as well, and they had a child around the same time Jordin was born. It was great! He and Jordin knew each other from the time they were babies and as Jordin was naturally awkward around other kids, it was wonderful that he always had a friend right next door.

We were at the church all of the time. Whether it was for Bible Quizzing practice for the kids, music practice, Wednesday night Bible study or Sunday services, we were there. Jereme and I wanted to be sure we raised our children around as much church as possible, just as our parents had raised us, so we rarely missed an opportunity to serve. Although, in our church, it was never called "serving" it was called "faithfulness" you showing up was pretty much just expected. If you missed, Barb would notice, and she never missed a chance to let you know she noticed. For years, I took it as her just looking out for my soul, then it became more of, I wanted to show up just so I wouldn't get hassled. Rob's mom would stand in the back every service and take attendance, so if by an off chance, Barb missed you not being there, the attendance taker would notice for sure.

We had lots of friends around us constantly, I should have felt like I fit in, but I didn't. We were so close to Rob and Barb by this time, we had shared a couple of family vacations with them and I was starting to hang out with Barb frequently during the day. Just like the rest of my life, I looked happy on the outside, but I was miserable on the inside.

It always seemed like something in my life was missing. Barb would get on to me all the time for jokingly saying I was going to hell. But, truthfully I wasn't joking. I sincerely thought I was. I just couldn't measure up to everything the church wanted me to do. It was stressful. I wasn't a demonstrative worshipper, I didn't agree with much of their modesty standards, I didn't witness enough, didn't give enough money; the list goes on and on.

The one standard of the UPC I did think I agreed with wholeheartedly was women not cutting their hair. It made me miserable that I agreed with this one. My hair was lifeless and dead from years of perms, curlers and blow drying it. It hadn't been cut since I was eight years old and it showed. I was limited to wearing it up most of the time because it just looked too thin and unhealthy down it was embarrassing. This aspect added to my feeling of ugly. Every day in the shower while I washed it, I would fantasize about somehow "accidentally" cutting it. I thought about leaning forward too far while cutting Jereme's hair, or even setting it on fire with a candle. Yes, I know my mind was a little twisted. You have to understand the level of desperation. If I were to cut it with scissors, on purpose, not only would my mother be upset with me and I would get kicked off the platform at church (this is what the church threatened to those who had a ministry such as singing or speaking as a tool to keep them in line. If you did something considered sin, you would have to sit out from your ministry and sit with the rest of the congregation for a certain amount of time, or basically until you had repented and came back to your senses), it would most importantly open up an opportunity for Satan to get to my family. Let me explain.

Around this time, I went to a ladies retreat that the speaker (who also happened to have written a book they were selling on the subject) made all of us women take our hair down and have a shout down prayer service, hair flying everywhere to celebrate the fact we had "power and covering on our heads". (1 Corinthians 11, I will expound more on this later) The speaker told us a story about a minister's wife who trimmed her hair and immediately her husband started having an affair, and her marriage and ministry fell apart. Her hair wasn't protecting her husband any longer simply because the ends of her "glory" had been cut off, thus causing him to commit adultery. She threatened us with the lives of our children and family members. Their very lives would be in jeopardy if we mistreated our God-given power as women and trimmed our hair. While I certainly did not dance and shout, (I am still me) I did take this message to heart and read her book. It made clear sense to me at the time. She laid out

38

her version of 1 Corinthians chapter 11 so flawlessly, to someone who has never questioned the validity of their church organization, she made valid points. So I could never quite bring my self to do it. I would just stand and look at my hair in the mirror with disgust.

As I have already mentioned, these conferences and conventions are a huge part of the UPC. They encourage every member from the age of eight on up to attend whatever convention pertains to your particular age group. In both of the UPC churches I attended, nearly everyone who could afford to would go. While it wasn't a salvation requirement, everyone who was anyone was there. Many times it felt more like a high school assembly then a church function. All of the important ministers would stick together like the popular jocks, their wives parading around in a posse like the blond cheerleaders. If you ever doubted which group you belonged to, you figured it out quickly while you were at a convention.

For this reason, it was kind of a thing in other people's eyes when Jereme and I went to a marriage retreat with Rob and Barb. When in reality, the only reason we were there, was to appease Barb. Due to the economy, and Jereme's job making some financial cuts, Jereme and I had been going through some financial difficulties. It was hard for me to work while taking Jordin to multiple doctor appointments, and not giving our ten percent tithes was not an option. Not giving at least ten percent, plus additional offerings was yet another an offense that could get you kicked off the platform. The mortification of that prospect backwardly seemed more humiliating than not having any money. Plus, we didn't want God to curse our money, as we were told would happen without the giving of our tithes.

We ended up having to file for bankruptcy, all the while not missing a payment to the church. This being said, Barb knew we were having money problems and when I told her we were skipping out on the retreat that year, she would not take no for an answer. That is her personality. Looking back now, I am certain she is a narcissist, but at the time, while I was annoyed with her pressuring me, the fact that they ended up letting us stay in their condo and having the church cover our food expenses, was flattering. I wish I would have seen this as a red flag.

Barb and I were very close friends, and I justified her behavior as just how she was. I hung out with her almost exclusively, and if I didn't agree with any part of our days out, my opinion would be immediately dismissed and she would do whatever it was she felt like at the time, all the while staying sweet and kind and twisting her idea into being something I wanted. I don't know how she did it. I could never get upset with her, and I always excused anything she did that bothered me somehow or another. She always had a way of getting exactly what she wanted. I can't even find the words to express how much of a professional bully she was. She would bully me in ways I didn't even realize she was doing it. She had an unbelievable air about her that was welcoming and kind, and seemingly very thoughtful. I watched her work her magic on several occasions to others as well. She would pressure people into purchasing her used items, cleaning her house, or even store clerks into giving her free or discounted goods or services. The amount of things I have witnessed this woman talk other people into is unreal. She had a real talent for manipulation. People didn't dare to cross her, as she was the pastor's wife and didn't have a problem using that position to keep you in your place.

It wasn't all bad being her friend. I would like to believe some part of our relationship was sincere. She had a special talent to give the perfect gifts and she always made me feel at home with her by her ability to have the right words to say at just the right time. When Jereme's dad passed away after a long illness, Barb and I were at the height of our friendship.

40

Jereme's parents had been pastoring a UPC church down south for several years and so his funeral was three and a half hours from our home. I didn't expect anyone of our friends to make the trip. I was wrong. Several people from our church came including Rob and Barb. They even got a hotel room in the little podunk town he was laid to rest in so they could attend the viewing and the funeral. I will genuinely be forever grateful for their support during this time.

Chapter 4

Questioning the UPC

The passing of Jereme's dad was a colossal turning point for not only the four of us but for my mother and sisters in law as well. Six months after the funeral, Jereme's oldest sister, Kay called and told us she was leaving the UPC. The vast array of emotions I felt after that phone conversation is indescribable. When a woman leaves the organization, an obvious outward physical change takes place, and when you are the one left behind, that change in their appearance can be very challenging to process. I know it sounds so extreme to say it is difficult to watch someone wear pants, makeup, jewelry, and cut their hair. To most people, these things are just natural. When you are raised UPC and see someone whom you have known their whole life who was also raised in the church do them, it can be incredibly emotional. You see, if you are truly a believer in the UPC's stance on such matters, you genuinely feel like your loved one would be going to hell.

This is where I was torn, I feared for Kay's eternal salvation. I was angry at her because now, not only had my children just lost a grandparent for the first time, they would see their aunt as on her way to hell and turning her back on the family traditions their grandfather taught. I viewed it as disrespectful since her dad had just passed. I was concerned for the wellbeing of my mentally fragile mother in law and Jereme's youngest sister who was still only fifteen years old. But on the flip side of all of this, I agreed with her reasons for leaving. As I already mentioned, Jereme and I weren't in wholeheartedly. We didn't believe most of the standards were Biblical; we simply followed them because our pastor said to do them and we didn't want to rock the boat by being disobedient. After all, obedience is better than sacrifice. (1 Samuel 15:22) But, I also trusted in the fact everything else that was taught in the organization was correct, so I almost did them as fire insurance, just in case they were right about the standards as well.

I turned to our pastor for answers to my questions. I wanted to know exactly why the standards were taught. He sent me screenshots from his phone of a UPC Bible study about the holiness standards I was questioning. I had pretty much memorized this study already after a lifetime of indoctrination, so it wasn't incredibly helpful. I was very disappointed with his lack of interest in my personal faith crisis. I was so lost and depressed and felt helpless watching my in-laws making what I felt to be decisions with serious eternal consequences. This is the point where what little faith I had hit rock bottom. I started researching churches in the area that taught the three-step salvation plan like the UPC but without the additional "standards". Hint, if you ever try to find one, there aren't any. At least in the area we lived. This fact lead me to believe, the UPC had to have everything correct, otherwise, there would be other church organizations out there teaching the true salvation plan. It was like a merry-go-round in my brain, emotionally exhausting.

After wrestling with these feelings for several months, the only thing I knew to do was to study. I felt like the best way to provide my children with the most stability was to get down to the nitty-gritty and search out for myself exactly where I stood on every topic; apparel, jewelry, hair, makeup. The idea of researching salvation never crossed my mind however, because I was certain we were in the clear on that aspect. I broached the subject to Jereme, who was immediately on board.

I didn't realize at the time, that while I had been oppressed and depressed for years about my religious bondage (although, I didn't realize that was where my sad feelings were coming from) Jereme had been fighting his own demons. While I felt like I was going to hell for my works not measuring up, he felt like his soul was doomed for the same yet very different reason. According to our pastor at the time, if you had not just repented for whatever punitive, unintentional sin you had presently committed and you died, or the rapture happened, you were sentenced to an eternity in hell.

For instance, let's say, you are a good Apostolic, and one day you get up early to pray, read your Bible, adorn yourself with perfectly modest clothing, get in your car to drive to work, someone cuts you off, you slip and say a curse word then have a heart attack. Off to hell you go, no chance to pass go or collect two hundred dollars. God is a God of judgment, not a big cosmic teddy bear in the sky as I once heard a minister put it. There are no leniencies to mess up, not even unintentionally.

This had Jereme convinced he was predestined to be damned. He confessed to me that he had been attending church and living it the best he could in front of our children, simply to give them a shot at heaven. We both agreed we

44

could not continue to live this way, we had to know for ourselves. We immediately began compiling a list of subject matters to search out.

After being raised in religious homes and Bible Quizzing, you would think we would have known how to study the Bible. We had no clue; we were completely lost on how to begin. We did know we didn't want to use any man-made materials, only God's Word. We wanted to go all the way back to the original Greek to make sure we had complete clarity on the modern-day definitions. We didn't want to trust anyone else's interpretations. Since neither one of us are foreign language or history majors, we enlisted the help of a sweet couple we knew. She was well educated in such things and he had gone to a UPC Bible college so we felt like together they were our best option to be unbiased and fair toward God's Word and not just our religion's beliefs.

Jereme and I decided we would begin with researching the idea women cannot cut their hair, and men are required to wear their hair short. I chose this topic because I firmly believed I agreed with the church's stance on the matter and thought it would be a quick topic to breeze through to begin our studies on the right note. I need to add the fact that while we were trying to be unbiased, ultimately our main goal was to find information to support our current situation. I sincerely thought the problem was within Jereme and me, not the UPC.

Since we were not using UPC materials, and since we were questioning the organization, we had to be rather secretive about our Bible studies. We didn't want anyone finding out because we didn't want it to get back to the pastors. I was actively involved in music and our family was very involved in other ministries, if word was to get around we were questioning things and searching for answers without using UPC published material, things definitely would have been said. There would have been people dragging us to the altar for prayer, giving us books to read, and lots and lots of judgmental comments. I simply did not want any of that.

The four of us met in a small room in the basement of the church two hours before service on Sunday mornings. We began breaking down the subject of hair, word by word, verse by verse in the original Greek text. I have already briefly touched on the UPC beliefs on this, but I will get into more detail now as I unfold how the Bible study progressed.

The UPC does not allow women to cut their hair at all and men are required to wear their hair above their collar. Most churches do not even allow men to have facial hair of any kind. This was true for the church we were attending. If you were a man and wanted to be used in any ministry, and especially on the platform for things such as music, you had to be cleanly shaven. The organization derives this belief from 1 Corinthians chapter 11. We will use King James Version here since these are the terms the UPC seems to gravitate toward.

The verses in question are these:

1 Corinthians 11:

4 Every man praying or prophesying, having his head covered, dishonoureth his head.

5. But every woman that prayeth or prophesieth with her head uncovered dishonoureth her head: for that is even all one as if she were shaven.

6. For if the woman be not covered, let her also be shorn: but if it be a shame for a woman to be shorn or shaven, let her be covered.

7. For a man indeed ought not to cover his head, forasmuch as he is the image and glory of God: but the woman is the glory of the man.

46

8. For the man is not of the woman, but the woman of the man.

9. Neither was the man created for the woman; but the woman for the man.

10. For this cause ought the woman to have power on her head because of the angels.

13. Judge in yourselves: is it comely that a woman pray unto God uncovered?

14. Doth not even nature itself teach you, that, if a man have long hair, it is a shame unto him?

15. But if a woman have long hair, it is a glory to her: for her hair is given her for a covering.

In this chapter, the apostle Paul states it is a shame for a woman to be shorn or shaven and a shame for a man to have long hair. It is also mentioned a woman's hair is her glory and in verse 10 it is stated: "For this cause ought the woman to have power on her head because of the angels." This is the very reason at the ladies convention I attended, the minister had all of the women take their hair down and pray. It is a common belief among UPC churches that this verse indicates women have some sort of angelic power associated with their hair.

I have heard ministers parallel the word "covering" used in this scripture passage with the blood covering God commanded the Israelites to put over their doors to protect them from the death angel in Exodus. Meaning, I have heard it taught, as a woman, your uncut hair is your family's covering to protect them and keep them safe from harm. Therefore, if you even as much trim your hair, you are opening the door to the devil taking down your family. Your children are unsafe, your husband may find other women attractive and cheat on you, your family will leave the church, you get the idea. The entire protection of her family

47

both physical and spiritual is all on the woman's shoulders. I have even heard women claim that the sick have received miraculous healings when they have laid their hair on them and prayed.

Come to find out, this teaching is just as erroneous as it sounds. The word covering in 1 Corinthians does not have any connection to the Old Testament. It most likely simply refers to a prayer veil, a common practice for women of that time period. The Greek words for shorn or shaven most likely translate into shaving the hair off completely just like sheering a sheep, not just trimming the ends, this was normal for prostitutes and harlots to do in Biblical times. Also, if there was any doubt left, verse 16 of the same chapter pretty much puts an end to the discussion. In this verse, Paul makes the statement:

16. But if any man seem to be contentious, we have no such custom, neither the churches of God.

It sounded to me like even Paul was saying, let's not argue about this guys, it really isn't a big deal!

By the end of four months of intense studying, learning the meanings of the original Greek text, and coming to the conclusion we could not possibly find any additional information we hadn't already considered, the four of us agreed it was indeed not Biblical to forbid women from cutting their hair, and the idea that women possessed some sort of magical protection from said practice, was far fetched, to say the least. We did end the study with both couples coming to different conclusions, however.

Jereme and I were flabbergasted something we believed in so strongly proved false, it was a hard pill to swallow. We went away from the study realizing how off base we were. The other couple had the opposite effect. Their consensus was there has to be a line. There has to be a standard of some

48

sort. The Bible indeed says women are to have long hair, and men short hair, so how would you ensure your hair was long enough to be considered long if you cut it. So, in their minds, the best thing to do to be sure your hair was long enough was to just not cut it.

I remember Jereme making the argument to them, "So if a man trims his hair just one time, is it considered short?" It's the same idea. If a woman can just trim her hair, and her hair not be considered long, then why would a man have to keep his hair above his collar? All he would need to do is trim it once or twice in his lifetime and it should be considered short. They did not like this comeback and didn't have anything to say to it. I respected them a lot (still do) and when they could not come up with a logical explanation to this dilemma, I was a bit shocked and upset.

I will never forget the day we came home from that last Bible study. I felt defeated, as if the floor had just been ripped out from under me. I had been so sure we were right. Even though I always despised the thought we were right because I hated my dead, lifeless hair, I entrusted in the belief that one day it would be worth it. My children would grow up happy and healthy and in the truth and my husband would come home every night all because I had been obedient and not cut off my "glory". I cannot even describe how betrayed I felt after having attended that conference and buying into the doctrine with everything I had in me. The sacrifice of my own self-esteem through the years was heart-wrenching.

Jereme and I began to face the hard fact if we were so wrong about the subject of hair, what about the other subjects we already doubted? While originally we were going to study out our list with the couple we researched hair with, after this revelation we decided to proceed on our own. We didn't want to create any rifts with them as we had ended with such differing opinions.

I also decided since I no longer felt it was Biblical to not trim my hair, I was going to do it! I was going to wait until we finished our studies, but after the initial shock wore off, I began to be cautiously excited about the prospect of finally having healthy hair.

Around this time, Barb decided the remedy to her uneven ends was to purchase expensive hair extensions to make her thigh-length hair appear thicker and healthier on the bottom. Obviously, I had not told her about our Bible study but one day after being over the top annoyed about her pushing me into buying those stupid extensions with her, I turned and looked at her and said, "I am not paying for those, I am going to cut my hair." I was as serious as I could be, but she thought I was joking. She started laughing and said, "Oh okay!" I just turned and walked off. That was my way of telling her, without actually getting into the subject with her. It was just easier to leave it with her thinking I was kidding.

Because Jereme and I were questioning things, I had taken a break from my position on the Sunday praise team until we had finished our studies. One Sunday morning, around Easter time, I was standing in the back of the sanctuary. A woman who always liked to get in on the good gossip as to make sure she could "pray for you" came to me and asked if I had gotten in trouble for something. I know my mouth dropped open. I knew people would be gossiping about my sitting on a pew instead of on stage, but to blatantly ask it to my face! I had no words. I just looked at her dumbfounded and said, "No, I did not get in trouble. I am exhausted from singing every single week for the past twelve years and I am taking a break." But this was confirmation of the reality of the church I was in. If I had shared the true reason I was sitting as I was having doubts, word would have spread like wildfire and every lady in the church would have been approaching me. I already knew what their answers to my questions would be, and I wanted more than manufactured, blanket, vague UPC textbook answers.

Toward the end of the following service, while the entire church was gathered around the front for prayer, (men on one side, women on the other as UPC services usually go) Barb took it upon herself to descend from her perch on the platform and approach me. Since I was not singing at this time, I was standing back safely a few pews from the altar behind most everyone else that was gathered around the front. She made me turn toward her and leaned into my ear said, "I see how happy you look on your social media posts with Marie. I don't understand why you aren't that happy to be around me, or the other church people. We are the ones who are your family. You should be just as happy to be around us as with her, and you never seem to smile here at church, I just don't understand why."

I was livid. Marie and I had been friends since childhood. Our friendship had survived teenage drama, out of state moves, marriage and children, I could not believe she was actually using my relationship with my best friend to try and guilt me! I was already spending most of my free time exclusively with her! She then proceeded to pray for me, praying to God that I would find happiness in the people who were always there for me. I just stood there motionless. I was afraid to even open my mouth as I was scared of what would have come out right there in the front of the church during prayer!

The truth of the matter was, she was right, I was happier around Marie than I was with her. In all actuality, my relationship with Barb was becoming a sore subject between Jereme and me. She was always calling me last minute to do things, and when we did go out, for some reason or another, no matter how many times I told her I had to be home for my kids to get off the bus, she managed to make me late. I can't even say how many times I had to call my

51

neighbor to get my kids off the bus for me because I was out with Barb and she was still shopping, or whatever we were doing. It was becoming more and more frustrating. Jereme felt like she was monopolizing my time away from family and other friends. It was starting to feel that way for me as well, so I had begun pulling back a little bit. Plus, I didn't want her to know we were researching the Bible. God forbid! It sounds so ridiculous now that I didn't want my pastor knowing I was reading God's Word!

All that little intervention did accomplish is make me want to leave even more than I already did at this point. Coming up with words to describe the sadness and depression I felt every time I walked through those church doors is difficult. I still thought it was me, which made it even more depressing. One of the scripture texts the UPC church I attended used to keep you from questioning their "truth" is Romans 1:26 and 28.

Using the King James Version as the UPC normally does, beginning with verse 26 the text reads:

26. Who changed the truth of God into a lie, and worshipped and served the creature more than the Creator, who is blessed forever. Amen

28. And even as they did not like to retain God in their knowledge, God gave them over to a reprobate mind, to do those things which are not convenient.

I had it ingrained in my mind that if I ever left the organization or the "truth as they call it, God would give me a "reprobate" mind and would never deal with my heart again and leave me in my sinful state forever. As miserable as I was, I kind of already thought that had transpired. I didn't feel God in the church services. Others would be shouting and praying loudly and I just sat there. I just couldn't bring myself to fake it anymore. It started to dawn on me how much the services are like a rock concert or a baseball game. The louder the music, the more the minister raised his voice, the more the people would respond. And the more response the music and the minister received, that was the measuring stick for how good the service was. So if the service leader wasn't getting the response he wanted, well, we just sang a faster song, or he stomped his foot a little harder and the "spirit" fell even more. As I sat in my pew and looked around, I realized how much the people there were like lemmings. Just following what the service leader said to do. He said to clap, they clapped, he said to raise your hands, they raised their hands. I hated every minute of it. I was sick and tired of songs that glorified the church and not God, I was exhausted with the messages constantly making you feel not good enough, but certainly better than the Catholics or Baptists down the road. I was sick of the pretentious, hypocritical backstabbing of the "rebels" who had left. I simply could not take any more of it.

At home, Jereme and I had quickly moved our research onto the idea women should only wear skirts or dresses. We got through this topic rather quickly as it did not take much studying to debunk it. In my experience, the verse the UPC references to enforce this standard is Deuteronomy 22:5 (KJV):

5. The woman shall not wear that which pertaineth unto a man, neither shall a man put on a woman's garment: for all that do so are an abomination unto the Lord thy God.

I have heard this verse taught in so many different angles. I think my favorite is: "If it was an abomination then, it's an abomination now! God is the same yesterday, today and forever!"

My eyes cannot possibly roll any further into my head!

53

Let's think about this logically for a minute, shall we? Let's face it; the UPC is stuck in the fashion of the 1940s. Which, I suppose makes sense, seeing as that is when the organization was first formed. In the 1940s, women predominately wore dresses, but not in the 7th century when the book of Deuteronomy was written. I am pretty sure the differences between male and female clothing was a lot more subtle back then when everyone wore robes. Also, I have read lots of research to support the idea; this law was aimed more toward women trying to wear men's war attire.

As for the abomination, God is the same argument mentioned above. Please do yourself a favor and read over Deuteronomy chapter 25. Verse 16 specifically uses the phrase:

16. For all that do such things, and all that do unrighteously are an abomination unto the Lord thy God.

This verse comes after the writer's rant about a law stating a man has to take his brother's wife, something about taking his shoe off and spitting in someone's face, blah, blah, blah. Obviously, we no longer abide by this law anymore either. And clearly, everyone has been unrighteous at some point or another.

And last, but certainly not least, this is Old Testament law! The UPC themselves will tell you we are no longer bound by the Old Testament rules and regulations, but for some reason, they make an exception for this particular verse. I think it is a little funny now, that this verse holds so much value with the UPC when they ignore the verse just six verses down that speaks of wearing garments of mixed materials such as wool and linen. And last time I checked, no one was stoning women in the street when they weren't found to be a virgin on their wedding night, yet another Old Testament principle found in the same chapter.

Yikes, that was hard to type without raising my blood pressure a little bit. I cannot believe I lived under this for so long! I cannot believe there are now, even as I type, thousands of other well-intentioned people out there living out this principle. Women who are under oppression day after day, year after year, decade after decade, and for what purpose?

Jereme and I then skimmed over the belief that women cannot wear jewelry and even quicker than the skirt argument was debunked, this idea came crashing down as well. Jewelry is often spoken of as a beautiful, positive thing in the Bible, not anything forbidden. I also felt it was entirely hypocritical that wedding rings were widely accepted in the organization, just as headbands and gaudy purses, but anything else was a sin. Who gets to decide these things? I was not previously convinced of this doctrine at all, but I did take the time to study it out, just to be sure.

One last thing we wanted to study is the UPC teaching about forbidding women to wear makeup. They teach it is vanity and harlot-like since Jezebel in the Bible wore makeup. Once I studied out the story of Jezebel, however, like the other standards the UPC teaches, this one carried no merit either. While Jezebel clearly was a questionable character in the Bible, and not at all a Godly woman, in the story that references her wearing makeup, she was getting dressed to meet the prophet. I'm sure she knew she was probably going to die, and just wanted to look her best, but nothing in the Bible mentions Christians cannot wear makeup. This is just one more instance where the UPC inserts their own teachings and tries to make the scripture line up.

By the time we had disproved all of the major holiness standards that the UPC teaches, Jereme and I were faced with the grim reality things we had been taught since childhood were brutally incorrect. We came to the conclusion we could not in good conscience pass on such flawed teachings to our children. The problem quickly arose, where would we attend church? The idea of not going anywhere was never an option to us, we wanted to raise our kids in a church, but we were so stuck on the UPC's three-step salvation plan, we felt trapped.

This is where God began leading us in very obvious ways. Although looking back now I can see where God's hand was upon us through all the doubts and questions.

I spoke with a childhood friend of mine who had left the UPC years before about a non-denominational church in the area her mother attended. I also knew of several other people who had left the organization that went there as well. I was aware her mom had been hardcore UPC at one point and I was curious as to what made her start attending this particular church. A church, that I might add, also used to be part of the United Pentecostal Church organization back in the 1980s. My friend gave me her mom's phone number and I called her immediately. I began asking questions about things I thought were important to me about a church. This woman is a saint. She was so patient and kind to me during that phone conversation, I am so thankful for her!

I asked her if the church was charismatic and lively like a UPC church. I wondered if people spoke in tongues loudly, clapped their hands, and ran the aisles during service. I wanted to know if my kids would be taught how important receiving the Holy Ghost was with speaking in tongues, I wanted to know if they were Oneness or Trinity, I asked about the baptism formula used. She calmly and graciously explained to me, the environment of services was a bit more controlled then the emotional hype of a UPC service. She explained people did speak in tongues there, but it was a bit quieter and only to themselves. She said she didn't know how they baptized and wasn't entirely sure about the Oneness or Trinity doctrine.

By the end of our conversation, I was very disheartened. My children were my number one priority and I wanted them to be in a church that had the same core values I held dear. While I was never the demonstrative worshipper, I had been taught how loud everyone got is how you knew God's presence was in a service. I couldn't believe she had no idea what way they baptized, as someone who had left the UPC, I assumed that would be something that would be important to her as well. Once again, I felt defeated. I had been excited about our conversation, thinking this could be my way out of my current situation. I had been talking to her in my car by myself and I remember hanging up with her as I was pulling into the garage. I just sat in my car and cried. I truly felt like God had abandoned me. Trudging into the house, I put the kids in bed and cried once more as I relayed my phone conversation to Jereme.

It was about five months after our initial searching began and we were getting into the habit of after putting the kids to bed, we would lie in our bed and read the Bible and discuss everything we had studied that day. Honestly, it is sad to admit, but this was the first time in our marriage we sought God together. This night was no different. As I laid down, not looking for anything in particular this time, simply searching for solace after my disappointing phone conversation, I opened my Bible to 1 Corinthians chapter 14. In this chapter Paul specifically makes the following statements:

"But all things should be done decently and in order."

"If, therefore, the whole church comes together and all speak in tongues, and outsiders or unbelievers enter, will they not say that you are out of your minds?

"The one who prophesies is greater than the one who speaks in tongues, unless someone interprets, so that the church may be built up."

Now, to be fair, I had heard portions of these verses taught on before, but never in context. It was as if a veil had been lifted from my eyes! No wonder I felt uncomfortable when I walked into the sanctuary at church where before service had even begun people were upfront pacing back and forth loudly speaking in tongues! There is no order in a typical UPC style service! Everyone just shouts out and does whatever they feel, pretty much whenever they feel like it. Like I have already said, this behavior always made me feel uncomfortable, but I always thought it was me. Reading this passage of scripture, opened my eyes to realize, even their service style isn't Biblical! Once again, principals I had been taught since a young child were proved false by God's Word itself. Attending the non-denominational church was now potentially back on the table! I was elated!

The final hang-up we had was the doctrine of salvation. The lady I spoke with about the church said something that made me roll my eyes a little. She used the phrase "accepting Jesus in your heart." This phrase is looked down upon and poked fun of a lot in my corner of the UPC. This is what those "easy believism" churches said when someone was supposedly "saved". I was always taught belief is simply the first "step" in the salvation process, something that was quickly passed over in obtaining the highest status of Christianity, becoming an "Apostolic" by speaking in tongues.

I am by nature a very impatient person, and being in limbo about our future, was nerve-racking for me. My mind raced constantly and all the what-ifs cruising through my brain made concentrating on anything else near impossible. What if we were to leave the church? How would this affect my kids? How would my family react? How would our neighbors respond, all our friends? By questioning the UPC, did I already have a "reprobate mind"?

58

I called Marie and told her everything that had transpired in the last few months. I just really needed a friend to talk to. I was leery of her response as she was still very much involved in her UPC church down south. She didn't have too much to say. I think the first time we had this conversation, it took her a little by surprise. We always said in times past if either one of us ever were to cut our hair, the other would slap them back into reality. Now, I was past questioning this belief and I straight up could simply not support it any longer. I was hoping she would be supportive, but was keeping in mind she would sincerely be concerned for my soul. It was a very odd place to be emotionally.

I began having difficulties leaving my house in UPC attire. Since I knew for certain I did not believe in the standards of the church, I felt as if I was lying to myself and others by dressing as if I supported it. This just added to my mental exhaustion and a crazy roller coaster of feelings. I was cautiously excited about the prospect of leaving the organization and the idea of going into a store and being able to find appropriate clothing without modifying it, but at the same time, my mind would wonder if we indeed were forced to stay in our current congregation because of salvational beliefs, would it be sinning to disobey my pastor by doing these things?

Another problem that was reeling in my mind was our neighbors. Not only did they attend our church, but our kids were close friends, and I was doing clerical work for his company part-time. I knew their extreme UPC stance about everything pertaining to religious legalism and knew it would create a rift if we were to ever leave. Would I still be able to keep my job? What about the kids' friendship? I felt so tired from being mentally and emotionally drained. UPC people tend to fear by befriending those who left, not only would that send a message you supported them leaving, you could potentially put yourself in a position of possibly "backsliding".

Jereme felt the best course of action would be to call the church we were considering directly. I was making dinner in the kitchen one evening when he walked in from work after his conversation with an elder. I impatiently waited for the kids to go to bed so we could have an opportunity to discuss what was said. Our kids knew we were studying things but had no idea we were considering leaving all they ever knew. Once again, I was heartbroken and disappointed by what was said.

Jereme asked the elder pertinent questions regarding the topics we felt were important to us. Their stance on the Trinity (mainly baptism formula) and salvational doctrine were a huge deciding factor for us in the prospect of leaving. The elder explained to Jereme when baptizing someone they said the phrase "in the name of the Father, Son, and Holy Spirit, which we know to be Jesus" and they believed salvation was upon belief, or grace-based, not works.

Jereme and I didn't know what to do. We felt so stuck. In the UPC, three-step salvation based on Acts 2:38 and baptism in Jesus' name only without mentioning the titles is taught to such extreme that you are terrified to believe anything else. You are programmed when you hear things such as "accepting Jesus" or "following Jesus" you automatically tune out the person who is speaking because they clearly do not know the "truth". Such phrases are irrelevant to the Apostolic believer because they feel they have gone above and beyond such elementary principles, again adding to the overall attitude of arrogance in the organization.

Once more, God showed up for us in a big way in the middle of our despair and desperation. The prospect of trudging through those UPC church doors any more brought me severe anxiety. I was almost to the point of just giving up

60

and not going anywhere. Jereme and I were so sure about the UPC's stance of salvation; we had not even anticipated studying the topic. However, God had other plans.

In the weeks following Jereme's conversation with the church elder, it seemed like everything I read indicated that possibly salvation could indeed actually come at belief. With my interest sparked, I began searching for answers in the same fashion I had studied out the standards. I began a list; in one column, verses that supported UPC three-step salvation, and the other column verses that supported salvation upon belief. I read the entire New Testament and any verse that contained the words, "eternal life", "saved", "salvation" or anything related to those words I added it to my list.

Do you know what I found? Verse after verse after verse supporting the act of salvation does indeed happen upon the sinner confessing and believing in Jesus! There were only maybe six verses (and I was rather lenient) in the other column supporting three-step salvation! The UPC uses the book of Acts as a basis for their whole religious structure by stating they are just like the church in the book of Acts. Interestingly enough, it turns out; yet again, that is indeed not the case. The ONLY verse in the entire New Testament that specifically asks the question, "What must I do to be saved?" is Acts 16:30 which reads: (ESV)

Then he brought them out and said, "Sirs, what must I do to be saved?"

That seems pretty direct and to the point to me. In this passage, Paul and Silas were speaking to the Philippian jailor. This guy had just witnessed some pretty amazing things and he was terrified he would lose his life because he thought the prisoners had escaped. What did Paul and Silas tell him? Verse 31 is their answer: (ESV)

61

And they said, "Believe in the Lord Jesus, and you will be saved, you and your household."

I could not believe what I was reading! My entire life I was taught Acts 2:38 was the response to the "what must we do to be saved?" question! But this seemed pretty straight forward right here! If more steps were indeed necessary for salvation, why in the world would Paul and Silas have left that man hanging? Why would they have only told him part of the salvation plan? That wouldn't have made any sense at all! I began looking at Acts chapter two in a whole new light.

Let's look at what Acts 2:37 and 38 actually says: (in the KJV of course)

37. Now when they heard this, they were pricked in their heart, and said unto Peter and to the rest of the apostles, Men and brethren, what shall we do?

38. Then Peter said unto them "Repent and be baptized every one of you in the name of Jesus for the remission of your sins and you shall receive the gift of the Holy Ghost."

Now, let's read verse 37 it the way I was always taught:

Now when they heard this they were pricked in their heart, and said unto Peter and to the rest of the apostles, Men and brethren, what shall we do to be saved?

Did you catch it? Three little words inconspicuously added to the end of the question! My whole church life I was taught that Peter's response in verse 38 was in reply to that question! What makes this even more disturbing is that Peter had already specifically used the phrase "shall be saved" in the same sermon back in verse 21 when he was quoting the prophecy of Joel.

62

Acts 2:21 (KJV) reads:

21. And it shall come to pass, that whosoever shall call on the name f the Lord shall be saved.

Wait, what? Peter had already told them who would be considered saved seventeen verses before verse 38! Why in the world would they be asking him how to be saved when he had already quoted to them their own Biblical prophesy telling them what the new salvation plan for after Jesus' death was going to be. Verse 37 was simply the Jews feeling guilty for crucifying Jesus and wanting to know where to go from this point. Peter is merely giving them follow up instructions, NOT a salvational command. This revelation was huge for me! Now, not only were the "holiness" standards of my church made up, and the church services conducted incorrectly, they were wrong about the fundamentals of salvation as well!

While God was showing me all of this new information throughout the course of a couple of weeks, unbeknownst to me, Jereme had been researching the historical side of the organization. God was directing him to some pertinent information from that angle as well.

Jereme began sharing his research with me and we were both astonished. He had discovered not only had the UPC edited early publications to change the way their founding fathers were portrayed, but we also found many documents that supported the idea the three-step salvation plan and stringent Oneness beliefs were not always an integral part of the doctrine of the UPC. When the church organization was first formed in the 1940s, it was a combination of two separate groups; the Pentecostal Church Inc. and the Pentecostal Assemblies of Jesus Christ, or the PCI and PAJC. The PAJC believed in three-step salvation, the PCI, salvation upon belief.

63

According to early documentation, (specifically the December 1945 issue of the Pentecostal Harold), the newly formed paper for the merged organizations would accept articles supporting either belief and vowed to not argue about it.

Additionally interesting for us to learn was, there was no mention of holiness standards in the original articles of faith from the 1950s, this was something that had been slowly added through the years. Another shocking discovery to us was, the words "for the remission of sins" were not added to the articles of faith until the 1970s, and only then were they added under the condition the word "for" would not be debated. What does this mean exactly? Let me try and break it down as simple as possible.

Since the merger of the PCI and PAJC included two groups that had very different salvational beliefs, the words "for the remission of sins" found in Acts 2:38 were not included in the original articles of faith. Why? Because the PCI believed Acts 2:38 should be translated to read like this:

*Then Peter said unto them, Repent and be baptized every one of you in the name of Jesus Christ **because** of the remission of sins…*

Meaning we are to be baptized because Jesus forgave our sins when we repented. The PAJC, however, felt the verse should be translated to read:

*Then Peter said unto them, Repent and be baptized every one of you in the name of Jesus Christ **in order to obtain** the remission of sins…..*

This is how Jereme and I had always been taught. You are baptized in order for your sins to be washed away. This belief places much significance in the act of baptism itself

64

and not the power of the blood of Jesus Christ. A verse that kept creeping into my mind at this point was Galatians 2:21:

21. I do not nullify the grace of God, for if righteousness were through the law, then Christ died for no purpose.

I felt numb, betrayed, lied to, and convicted for placing my trust in my own actions and not the act of the cross. Over many days the realization that everything we ever knew was completely false, puffed up, and elaborated upon by our so-called leaders was crushing. Words cannot even begin to describe how I felt. My entire life was a waste. I was humbled when I began to think about all of the Christians in my life I had judged because they were not a part of this organization I had supported. I felt foolish, duped, and very, very small. The realization of Galatians 2:21 flooded my heart. If I had relied on my own works, my own goodness as my salvation, I had rejected God's grace. If there were anything I could do on my own to assist in my salvation, Christ had died for no purpose. Even now I start to tear up thinking about all of the sacrifices I made in the name of pleasing God or being holy. How arrogant was I to think there was anything more I could add to God's amazing grace or Christ's sacrifice? God did not call us to look different by appearance, he called us to love and be known for our love.

Jereme and I were on the same page. We simply had no choice but to leave our current church. We could no longer support any of the teachings there and we did not want to confuse our children by attending a church we did not agree with. The idea of leaving although appealing was daunting. I was acutely aware of how everyone would think about us. All of the people we knew and loved, including my family, would genuinely be concerned for our souls. They would feel we had left the "truth" and be bound for hell. We would no longer be viewed as friends. They would view us as souls to be saved, their personal mission field.

It is a common misconception within the UPC that the people who leave, do so out of rebellion. While I suppose that could be true for some, I began to realize how small-minded that belief was. From the beginning, we had wanted nothing more than to reaffirm our childhood beliefs by studying out God's word. Instead, God guided our studies from the get-go and had shown us in indisputable ways the errors of our current doctrine.

I will never forget the last Sunday we attended our UPC church as members. I had been asked to sing that morning in the ensemble that I held very dear to me. As I previously mentioned, I sat myself down from the music while we were studying things out for a couple of months, but they were short-handed this particular morning and needed me. This was one area where it was very difficult to let go. Those people were my family and they needed me and my commitment. The song we were singing this particular day was a song I shared the lead with another lady. Whichever one of us felt like doing it was normally how it worked. This week, one of my close friends who was the leader of the ensemble asked the other lady to do the song. Typically, I would not have cared a bit, she is a wonderful singer, and being the lead is not my favorite thing anyway. This morning it hit me. They did not in fact "need" me up there. The show would go on with or without me! This was a giant weight off my shoulders! I most certainly did not want to put my friends in a bind by leaving. I had such an instant peace about it, I know it was a God thing.

While I was sitting on the platform waiting for the service to begin, Barb came up behind me. She touched my shoulder and said, "good morning." I do not know what it was about that gesture this particular day, but with our relationship being a bit rocky, and the fact I knew this could potentially be one of our last Sundays, I lost all control. I ran off the stage, down the back steps, and out the door. I had never before in my life had a panic attack until this moment. Jereme found me hyperventilating in the parking lot behind the church. I told him I simply couldn't do it anymore. I could not go back. My poor husband, he is always my rock. He just hugged me and said, "You don't have to honey. Let's make this our last Sunday".

I pulled myself together and walked back inside. By then, service had already begun without me in a microphone, (the show indeed did go on). Three songs in, in the middle of offering, Barb descended from the platform in her usual style and made a beeline to the back of the church where I was sitting. She asked me what was wrong and I simply didn't answer. I couldn't. I had nothing to say. She had been slowly pushing me to the brink of insanity and what I had suspected was made abundantly clear by my body's immediate, uncontrollable reaction when she simply told me good morning. Thankfully, she eventually left and walked back to her position on the platform. I sat there the rest of the service, oblivious to anything else around me, just trying to make it through the next hour and a half.

Because our children were having their last Bible Quizzing practice of the season that Sunday evening, we attended church that night as well. I didn't speak to anyone, just sat on my phone trying to block out everything. That was the last time I stepped foot into that church as a member.

Chapter 5

Transition to Freedom

The next week was crazy! My step sister and nephews were in town, the last Bible Quizzing Tournament for the kids was that weekend, and it was Fathers Day! I took the kids to their tournament Friday night and Saturday, attempting to act as normal as possible. It's so funny now, I was terrified someone may catch on to our plans, but the only people we had confided in were my parents and even they didn't know exactly what we were doing yet! Telling everyone was something I felt needed to be done correctly and carefully. I wanted to salvage every relationship that I could, so it needed to be done gently and at the right time.

I convinced my stepsister who went to cosmetology school years ago to cut my hair for me. I did not want to be embarrassed by going to a salon. I mean, really, what was I going to say when they saw my ridiculously damaged hair? I would have been mortified! Not to mention, I assumed this would be an emotional experience for me, I fully anticipated tears. Although my sister had grown up around the UPC, she had never been involved in the church herself having lived with her mom in another state. She did, however, appreciate the heaviness of the decision. I planned on her cutting it the evening the Bible Quizzing tournament ended. It was perfect timing as my parents were out of town for a wedding. I told Jereme before I had her cut it, we needed to inform my stepbrother who lived in town and was a licensed UPC minister.

My poor brother, while my husband is gifted at many things, sometimes wording things as to not come out so bluntly is not his talent. We were all sitting at a very loud restaurant and Jereme just nonchalantly leaned over and said: "so, we are leaving (our church name) and going to start attending (new church name)". My brother thought he was joking and started laughing. Jereme looked at him and said, "Dude, I'm serious". My brother just responded, "Okay, we will discuss this later". I do feel a little bad about this interaction. Probably wasn't the best timing to inform him of a major life decision!

After dinner, we went to my mom's house, where my sister was staying, and I told Jocelynn I was going to cut my hair. I told her, if she wanted to, she could trim hers as well, but it was her choice. I certainly wasn't going to make her if she didn't feel comfortable, but I informed, her father and I no longer believed it was wrong, so I was going to do it. She was a bit shocked because as far as she knew, we were still UPC.

We pulled a chair into my mother's kitchen and dug around for some scissors. It was surreal. I knew my mom would downright have a heart attack if she had any clue as to what was taking place in her kitchen, so I swore all of my nephews to secrecy. As I mentioned, I fully anticipated feeling guilty and emotional, but my experience was the exact opposite! Once I saw the pile of dead, disgusting split ends on the floor, I was relieved! She had only taken a few inches off, which is nothing when your hair is to your butt, but holy cow, what a difference! I felt light, excited like I could breathe and a burden was taken off of me! It was at that moment I began to realize what oppression I had been living under for so long. Jocelynn opted to trim hers as well, and loved it! It was an amazing evening and I am so happy my sister was in town to do it for me!

When I got home that evening, I could not stop staring in the mirror at my hair! I loved it! It was nowhere near healthy, but at least the ends were even. It was a very different feeling looking at myself this time. No tears, no oppression, just pure joy and happiness! I had no idea what the future held, but I knew it had to be better than the past! I felt genuinely happy.

The next day was Father's Day and we had already planned to go to a baseball game in the afternoon with my family, so when we were not at church that morning, it wasn't really noticed. As fate would have it, we ran into my mom's boss and his family at the baseball game and I was so concerned they would notice my trimmed ends! They insisted on taking a picture with us and since my hair was in a braid to my side I was terrified they would send the picture to my mom and she would notice for certain! My fears went unfounded, and the rest of the day went on with no hiccups!

That evening, I decided to call and tell my friend Marie what I had done. We were leaving for vacation that week, and I knew I would be posting pictures on Facebook, I did not want her to find out that way. If anyone would notice a few inches off the bottom of my hair it would have been her. It seems weird now to think I had to forewarn my friend I got a hair cut, but it was necessary. I was so anxious that our leaving the UPC would affect my relationship with Marie. She was so incredibly gracious however, and made the conversation as easy as possible. She cried, I cried, but ultimately she told me we would remain friends no matter what. She loved me and accepted me no matter where I attended church. It was beautiful, a true testament to her character. The only request she had was for me to send her pictures of myself so she could be mentally prepared for the next time she saw me. I understood knowing how awkward it can be to watch someone transition out of the organization.

Next on the list were my mom and stepdad. They were a bit trickier. I called my mom while they were on their way home from the out of town wedding they were attending and told them we had decided to leave. It was awful. These people were my children's grandparents, their Bible Quizzing coaches, their children's church leaders. Church was very much a family affair for us. Every Sunday afternoon my kids would ride home with Grandma and Papaw and we would eat lunch at their house with my brother and his family. Our leaving rocked the boat a lot and it was a difficult conversation to have. They were curious as to why we decided to go this road and were concerned we were backsliding. They thought by us leaving the UPC, we would leave God altogether. I don't think it came as a big surprise to them because we had confided in them our questions a few times along the way, but the hurt was still very real. I felt so guilty. They would be genuinely worried about our eternal damnation and that of their grandchildren. They were devastated, and we could not tell them all of the why's right then as that would be a long conversation to have. There were many tears and we promised to have a more in-depth conversation with them when we returned from vacation.

The next day we went over to my mom's house to tell everyone goodbye before we went out of town. My mom just stood in the garage and cried. It was terrible and made me feel so guilty. Leaving for vacation knowing how she felt was difficult.

Everyone else on our list would have to wait until we returned from our trip. Rob and Barb had been out of town as well, and we did not want anyone else to know before they did. We were trying to do it right and make sure we told them ourselves, news this big spreads through a small church like wildfire. Also, we were meeting a family from our church for a few days while we were on vacation, so we were trying to tread lightly. We did not want to make vacation uncomfortable for anyone.

We were planning on driving to Florida, so Jereme and I decided we would tell our children during the hours we were on the road. In preparation for this discussion, I put together a small Bible study to let the kids read over if they had any questions. I wanted to be as prepared as possible because I knew this would be huge for them. Not only were they going to be leaving all of their friends, and family, they were old enough to have been indoctrinated by the church and felt like they had the "truth". I was also worried about Jordin's social anxiety. How would he respond to being in a big church that was ten times the size of our previous church?

About an hour or two into our trip, Jereme and I felt like the timing was right to tell the kids. We explained how we had been studying things out and felt God was telling us to leave and go to a different church. I told Jocelynn it would be her decision if she wanted to cut her hair or wear pants. I certainly was not going to force her into doing anything she didn't feel comfortable with. We also made a point to let them know they could visit the old church with Grandma and

Papaw anytime they wanted, except on Sunday mornings when we would be at our new church together as a family. We told them they could stay in touch with their friends, go to camp and anything they wanted to do so they could remain friends.

They were shocked, but they handled it like champs. There were lots of tears and questions, Jereme and I were honest and tried to explain things as clearly as possible for them. Once the initial shock wore off, they started asking questions about our new church. Unfortunately, since Jereme and I had never been, we didn't know the answers. We just knew God was calling us there and we were going by faith. We went through the little Bible study I had put together, I was really glad I had taken the time to write everything down. We told them to not say anything to the family we were meeting up with as to not make vacation bad for anyone. They completely understood. Jocelynn was thirteen at the time and Jordin was nine, so they were old enough to get it. Jocelynn decided immediately she was okay with wearing pants and cutting her hair. Let's face it, she was in middle school, the age where everyone is awkward and nobody fits in. I was happy for her that she would be able to be herself without hiding behind the dress code of the UPC.

We ended up stopping at a huge Old Navy when we arrived at our vacation destination. Jocelynn and I bought our first pairs of shorts for vacation. Long ones, of course, I still couldn't bring myself to buy short ones. I remember standing in the fitting room close to tears because I had zero ideas about what I was doing. I knew how to buy skirts and dresses, but had no clue how to wear shorts and pants. What kind of shirt will look good, what shoes? It was all so overwhelming! I did know I was excited to not feel guilty about wearing a swimming suit at the beach! I was a little bit rebellious, as I have already mentioned, and already did that, but this time, I didn't have to feel like I was breaking the rules by doing so! I still only wore a tank on top with shorts on the bottom. I thought I could never be one of those women who let it all hang out in a bikini.

Another problem I was facing was how my butt looked in shorts. I had always been taught it was the woman's responsibility to dress a certain way for men to not lust after her. Men are visual creatures and just couldn't help themselves from thinking perverted thoughts if the woman was dressed immodestly. I was concerned about causing a man to stumble, or someone besides my husband lusting over my body. I had a terrible body image because of that teaching. I was ashamed of any curves I had and felt the need to hide them completely.

Our vacation was amazing. I think that was one of the best vacations we have ever taken. We bonded as a family in ways we hadn't before. It felt like the four of us taking on the world together. The kids did great when we met up with the other family and didn't let anything slip. After that, we went to a beach resort and stayed there for a few days.

Sitting by the pool, watching my kids swim, smelling the ocean breeze, and drinking mango margaritas was the absolute perfect way to desensitize myself from all of the stress I had been feeling for the last two years. My father in law's sickness and passing, my sister in law leaving the organization, and all of the searching and studying I had been doing had taken an emotional toll on me. All I could think in those moments was "how could it be this easy? How could living for God, be this simple that it did not require standards of dress and extensive rules and regulations?" I was in awe at the leading hand of God in my life over last few months and felt such freedom words cannot even begin to do justice.

Jereme and I would just look at each other periodically and say, "I can't believe it is this easy!" But it was! It was like we had broken out of a lifetime of prison after realizing the door had been unlocked the entire time! I felt like an adult for the very first time in my life. I was free!

While we were in Florida, Jocelynn and I decided on a rainy day we would go get our hair trimmed professionally. I don't know what I was thinking, doing that in a town I wasn't familiar with, not to mention, I had never even been to a salon in my life except to get a perm! Like I had feared initially, the lady who was cutting our hair was disgusted with mine and made many snide remarks about how damaged it was. She told me there was nothing she could do with such a bad cut and made me feel hideous. She didn't know my story, so I'm sure she was just shocked anyone could let their hair get so damaged. But the reality of a lifetime of bondage came rushing back to me and I couldn't get out of there fast enough. I made a mental note to tell the next person that did my hair at least part of my history just so maybe they would keep their negative comments to themselves.

All good things come to an end at some point, and after two weeks of vacation, we headed home to reality. As we got closer and closer to home, the dread of what lay ahead was beginning to set in. All of the people we would have to tell, and what would be said to us was not easy to think about. Like I said before, they would be genuinely concerned for our souls, and even though I knew better, it still was difficult for me to put my loved ones through that. Imagine if you were to watch your best friend cliff dive off the side of the Grand Canyon without any ropes. That would be the feeling our friends would have toward us. Thinking we had just committed spiritual suicide. I suspected there would be many tears, prayer meetings, and discussions about us behind our backs. I was hoping I was wrong, I hated the thought.

After we had been home for less than twenty-four hours, Jereme called Rob. He explained to him everything that had happened and told him we would no longer be attending his church. Jereme said he could tell Rob was crying as he said, "We will get together to schedule an intervention". Jereme was so brave to be the one to have that discussion; I know I couldn't have done it. I regret now the decision I made to not contact Barb personally at that moment. I should have had the courage to call her myself, but I just couldn't bring myself to do it. I knew her reaction would be more than I could handle, and I just couldn't bear it.

Instead, I went next door to tell my neighbor. That meeting went as horrifically as I imagined it would. She was so very angry with me. She asked if I would be cutting my hair. I told her I already had and the look that came across her face was that of sheer terror. She honestly felt I was putting my family at risk by trimming the ends. She asked what church we would be attending and I told her. She did not like my answer, she said, "They baptize in the titles!" I explained to her what the elder told us, "They say, I baptize you in the name of the Father, and the Son and the Holy Spirit, which we know to be Jesus". Stumbling over her words she said, "Well that is wishy, washy and just covering all the bases!" By this point, I was getting a bit steamy at the way this conversation was going so I replied: "Well, that is the way Jesus said to do it in Matthew 28:19!" This just angered her even more, so she began attacking the pastor and how he himself was a "backslider". She threw in that she felt I was dooming my children to hell, and she hoped an angel would visit me every day to show me the error of my ways. She ended her rant by saying she would pray that I would feel so much conviction I would never sleep again.

I trudged home and just cried. There was nothing else to do.

My conversations with my other close friends went better than my neighbor's. They were all very sad but vowed to stay friends with me. No one else blatantly called me out or said I was going to hell until Barb finally broke her silence and texted me.

I knew things between Barb and I would be shaky, but I had no idea some of the things that would be said, or how they would affect me so badly. She said she felt nauseous when her husband had told her we were leaving. She thought she knew me, but clearly, she didn't. She said she felt lied to and deceived because the person she thought she had been friends with didn't exist. I tried in desperation to explain to her, I was still the same person, and us leaving didn't have anything to do with her personally. Even though our friendship had been up and down over the last year, I still felt like she would continue to be friends with me, or at least on speaking terms.

I was stunned the first time Barb called my friend Marie. They did know each other, but it wasn't like they were friends or anything. Barb warned Marie about who she talked to and hung around and how they can affect her spiritually. She told her she was concerned for her since Marie's church at the time was experiencing some pastoral difficulties and Barb said she was troubled for her soul. She also managed to include in the conversation how she felt sorry for my mother, the poor woman just cried and cried at the altar praying for her wayward children. I was livid. How dare she not only try and convince my best friend not to talk to me but to throw my mother under the bus as well! She knew good and well Marie was going to tell me what she said to her, she knew it would get back to me. Such guilt tactics! It was one thing for her to say things to me to my face, but to try and manipulate others, I couldn't believe it.

I called my mom and set up a time for the four of us to sit down and have a church discussion. My mom and stepdad came over and Jereme and I laid everything out for them. The UPC's history, the scriptures we discovered, everything. Surprisingly, my parents didn't argue or try to convince us otherwise, they were rather quiet and listened to everything we had to say. They weren't in the right place to take it to heart, however. If you aren't searching for yourself, you tend to listen with a closed mind. But they seemed to handle it well at the time. What Barb had said about my mom being so sad at church haunted me and I apologized to my mom profusely. While I was mad at Barb for using my mother to guilt me, I did still feel bad for my mom. I had seen the mothers of "backslidden" children weep and wail at the front of the church, and I did not like the idea of my mother being one of them.

Before we attended our new church for the first time, I decided I was going to go shopping. I did NOT want to walk in looking UPC in the slightest bit. Jereme took me to several stores, and I tried on so many pants! I had no idea what I was doing or what my style was, so the experience was incredibly overwhelming. I finally settled on some grey dress pants that were a size too large because I was paranoid about anyone seeing too much of my curves. I had to pull those dumb things up all day long, but at least I wasn't in a skirt!

Walking out of my house the first year or so after we left, knowing that my next-door neighbors would be judging every stitch of clothing from here on out was nerve-racking. I was already unsure of my style, but worse, I knew what it was like when others left the church. Honestly, I think it happens mostly out of jealousy, but people judge you and gossip about how unflattering your new look is. Even if you look like an absolute model, it doesn't matter, they will bash you. I know it happens, I am sad to admit I did it myself!

That Sunday after vacation was the first time we walked through the doors of our new church. All four of us were nervous about this transition and I just prayed that if it was God's will for us to attend there permanently, we would know without a shadow of a doubt, and everyone would have a good experience. Jordin teared up as he was being escorted to Sunday school, but he went like a champ. Jocelynn's age group did not have a class that week, so she sat in the main sanctuary with us. Service was much quieter and more reserved than what we were used to, and the preaching much calmer, but I took away something from that service. Years later, I still remember the message that was preached, and for me, that speaks volumes. My entire life I maybe remember a handful of messages, and none of them challenged me to be a better person, but this one did! The minister spoke on love. A topic I had rarely heard preached about before, but I left the church that morning feeling refreshed and inspired.

We all loved it! Even Jordin! We felt very welcomed, I enjoyed the fact it didn't seem like a fashion show with everyone trying to outdo one another with ridiculously over the top formal outfits like what I had been accustomed to in the UPC. It was very much come as you are, and everyone looked normal. I appreciated the anonymity of no one knowing if I was a visitor or not simply from my appearance. It was nothing but a positive experience all around. I was relieved. A new chapter in our life had begun.

Chapter 6

Life on the Outside

As time went on, it became more and more apparent to me how we had been friends with people simply out of convenience. We are all guilty of it. We were in contact simply because we saw each other at church on weekends and Wednesdays. I started to feel more and more depressed as days would go by without me talking to anyone. I would reach out and people would usually respond, but it was always me making the effort. But I was determined to stay friends with them, even if that was the case. I thought, if I just kept trying, things would eventually go back to the way they were before. I was lonely all the time. It is such an unusual feeling, to be so happy deep down, but lonely at the same time. While I didn't look at myself in the mirror and loathe my image any longer, I felt empty from lack of friendship.

The only person in the UPC whose relationship didn't skip a beat was Marie. She was amazing. I leaned on her a lot for support and a listening ear. I did have to be careful about what I said to her, as I did not want to be viewed as proselytizing. She is entitled to her own beliefs the same as I am and contrary to what Barb thought, I did not want to sway her away from her church at all if she was happy there.

The one time people actually would reach out to me was when they had a good church service. They would text me telling me how they missed me, or that my mother had been crying. I know they sincerely thought they were helping the situation, but all it did was make me feel like crap and vow to never go back to that church because it would be out of guilt. Every time I would ask my mom about what they said, she wouldn't respond. All she could do was cry. It was awful.

Trying to describe the emotions I felt during the first year or two after we left can only be described as grieving a death. I went through a plethora of feelings and they would change from day to day. I would have moments of incredible happiness and thankfulness, followed by days of extreme loneliness and depression. While I wasn't crying in the shower about the prospect of living in bondage forever, I was acutely aware of all of the times I had and felt angry I had taken so long to make a move to better the situation. I felt betrayed by my church and hated that my extended family was still stuck there. I was excited my children would grow up free, but sad they had to experience any of that lifestyle in the first place.

It truly felt after we left, my childhood stick figure nightmare was coming to fruition once again. Not with my father or close family this time, but with my friends. There

I was once more, standing in the middle of a crowded room screaming at someone to cast a kind eye or word toward me, and everyone was crossing their arms, looking away, judging me.

Unbeknownst to me at the time, my mother started feeling the same way at church. One service Rob was telling her how he missed my husband on one of his yearly preaching outings Jereme would usually accompany him to. My mom said, "Well, why didn't you invite him? He probably would have gone." Rob's response was, "I don't think I should be around him right now." My mother was floored and crushed. Here was the pastor of her church, who was supposed to be watching over souls and he was too good to be seen in public with a "backslider"! My mom started to withdraw and pull herself out of any ministries she was involved in. Watching my mom go through the rejection on my behalf was just as heartbreaking as the realization all of my friendships were essentially over.

Over the course of the first summer, after we left, many changes took place for me. One of them being, Jereme bought me my first necklace! I was thirty-three years old and had never worn one! It wasn't expensive, it was just a cheap little thing, on it hung a simple leaf. The card it came on read: "turning over a new leaf". It was perfect! I wore that little necklace all the time! I also got my ears pierced! I felt so stupid sitting in that chair as an adult getting my ears pierced for the first time, but it was liberating! My cousin and my aunt took Jocelynn and me and we had the best day! We also went shopping and my cousin talked me into buying my first pair of skinny jeans. I was hooked! They looked amazing on me and it felt good to have someone encourage me that it was okay to show my curves. It was also nice to have someone find the right size for me! The pants fit me beautifully I loved them! I was finally for the first time figuring out my style and who I was. I had no one to be happy for me other than my cousin and my husband. Everyone else I knew would have condemned me for feeling so free in a pair of jeans. But I didn't care, I felt liberated! It is astonishing how looking good, makes you feel better overall. I had never had that feeling before. I was beginning to feel pretty for the first time in my life.

I remember walking into my mother's house the first time after getting my ears pierced. She just turned and looked at me and said, "so you gonna get a tattoo next?" My sassy response was, "not today!" She then led me downstairs away from everyone and sat me on the couch and lectured me about how I was looking "worldly" now with my pants and my earrings, and she was concerned I would walk away from God because I had crossed lines. I calmly sat there and let her speak, rolling my eyes to myself in my head. I knew she had good intentions and I felt bad she was in such bondage herself.

That fall, Jocelynn had a birthday party. Since we had just started attending our new church a few months before, she didn't know anyone there to invite just yet. She also still wanted to keep in touch with friends from our old church, so she invited several girls including Rob and Barb's daughter. I honestly don't remember the whole fiasco about which girls were having issues, but I do remember it was an ordeal. Parents were unsure if their daughter should come to our house or not. Barb was a huge part of that controversy, by using her role as the pastor's wife to spread fear to others that we were trying to pull their child over to the dark side. As it ended, several girls did come, but not after much drama, which hurt Jocelynn's feelings big time. I think it was just a few months after her party, Jocelynn decided she had had it with the drama. One girl asked my daughter if her parents held a gun to her head and made her cut her hair, then publically shamed her on social media for wearing makeup to a dance. Another girl was giving her a hard time about seeing her out in a necklace. Jocelynn ended up having to block several of those girls from her social media and honestly went into her own season of depression. I would be amiss not to include my children in the feelings of loneliness, they too experienced deep wounds from other children, who I'm certain were just repeating things they heard their parents say.

Winter came and went and by the next summer, Jordin was missing his friends and wanted to go to camp with our old church. Of course, we allowed him to go, I always told my kids anytime they wanted to go with their friends they could. That was a mistake on my part. By now, we were a full year out and our kids were getting pretty grounded in our new beliefs about salvation and baptism and saw the differences between what the UPC taught and what the Bible says on the subject.

When I picked Jordin up after a week of camp, he got into the car and lost it. I felt like a dreadful mother! He just cried and cried. By the time he calmed down enough to tell me what happened, I was heartbroken for him. According to Jordin, he was ditched frequently by the boys, treated rudely by one child in particular whose parents used to be our friends, one child asked him about why his parents made him leave, and to top it off, he had a horrific situation at the prayer altar.

Apparently, a boy who was a mutual friend of Jordin and our neighbor's son was praying at the altar one evening. This child's parents did not attend a UPC church, he was just visiting the camp that night. Jordin was praying with him and the boy told them he had received the Holy Ghost. Jordin was ecstatic and happy for him! My neighbor's son started arguing with him saying he had not received the Holy Ghost because he had not spoken in tongues. A small quarrel ensued between the boys and my neighbor who was also visiting the camp for the evening walked over. Her son proceeded to tell her what they were bickering about and she told the child who was so very happy that Jesus had come into his heart, that he had not received the gift of the Holy Ghost and was therefore not saved. That child and Jordin were so upset. Jordin looked at me while he was tearfully telling me that story and said, "Mom! How could she say that to him? She isn't God, she doesn't know if he was filled with the Holy Ghost or saved!" I was so proud of my son for knowing the doctrinal errors of the church, but heartbroken he had to watch his friend get deflated by someone's ignorance. That was the last time either of my children went to a UPC camp.

At this point, I was still working for my neighbor's small business. It was seemingly going uneventful despite the tiffs with his wife. I had been very concerned about his reaction when we left, but he took it much better than his wife did to my face. It hadn't affected our work relationship; I thought, until one day out of the blue one of Barb's other close friends contacted me. I was immediately suspicious since Barb had continued to harass Marie about our friendship and I thought she was asking questions because Barb wanted her to stir up jealousy on my part. She wasn't however; she was searching for herself. She was questioning things and was curious about how we came to the decision to leave. I won't go into her story, as it is hers to tell, but one thing that came to light during the process of talking to her over the next several months was the fact my neighbors had been asking the church to help them pray we would move. I was devastated. I knew there was talking going on behind our backs, I had expected it. But to have someone we were so close to be nice to our faces and behind our backs tell people they were concerned our kids would be a bad influence on their children, then to top it off, actually have people pray we would move was an indescribable betrayal.

Even before we left the organization, our neighbors were a lot stricter about following the rules than we were, and I always made sure we respected their views in front of their children. I did not allow my son to watch certain movies, play with certain toys, and such like when he was around their kids. My children also knew to discuss church was strictly off-limits. I was crushed. I assumed we had been being very proactively respectful of them. How could they enlist others in a vendetta against us? I thought since no one had told me until now, my friends that I had known for years were siding against us.

I told Jereme I couldn't do it anymore. I could not pretend to still be their friends or to work for him when they clearly did not respect us at all. He was supportive of my decision and I started looking for another job. I contacted a realtor as well because if they wanted us to move that badly, I was happy to oblige. I also immediately called Marie for emotional support as usual.

She was enraged for me, and like any good friend went straight to Facebook to unleash her feelings. I say that sarcastically, but yet, thankful she stood up for me. My neighbor quickly put two and two together and realized she was talking about them specifically and right away retaliated. Out of sheer anger, he called Marie a bad friend to his wife and said ridiculously hurtful things to her out of nothing but true spite for Jereme and me. It was crazy. I was infuriated.

I marched myself straight across the yard and banged on their door at 8:00 AM on a Saturday, Jereme following me shaking his head the entire way. "Just stay out of it" is his motto, but I couldn't take it anymore. It had been a year after we left, and I could not handle the drama for one more second. It's funny really, how I had allowed myself to be under the illusion things would be different for us. Surely Jereme and I wouldn't be talked about the way I had always heard other people who had left be torn apart. Surely we had been closer than that. Ugh, such naivety on my part!

"This ends now!" I shouted as they stood in their doorway in their pajamas. I have to think on some level they knew this confrontation was coming. I also think they wanted it to happen. I laid everything out and asked them straight up if they had been praying for us to move. At first, they tried to deny it. Then after me revealing how I knew, they admitted to it but insisted they no longer felt that way. I told them I didn't believe that as I knew they felt like we were going to hell. They tried denying that belief as well until Jereme called them out on it and asked them directly if they indeed thought that. Their response was, "you have left the truth, so yes, we feel like you are going to hell." Not that I need anyone's approval, I had already proved to myself by this point I could make my own decisions, but that still stung a little. My ever-gracious husband ended the conversation with prayer, but I knew I could never trust them again.

As I was preparing for our upcoming summer vacation, I happened to run across Barb at the grocery store. She pretended like she didn't even see me. I felt like between this interaction and what we had just experienced with our neighbors, I was through with trying to maintain past relationships. I was just too emotionally exhausted from the continual rejection and backstabbing. It wasn't worth the stress. This was the beginning of the end for me.

We left for vacation the next week and on the two and a half week drive across the country I applied for jobs. By the time we returned, I had an interview lined up at an optometrist office. We also officially put our house on the market.

Chapter 7

Revelation of Grace

Being about a year out of initially leaving the organization, we were still in awe of the freedoms we were experiencing. By this point, I was becoming more comfortable in my own skin and was beginning to experiment more and more with clothes. I wasn't as adamant about the length of Jocelynn's shorts and was allowing her to wear some sleeveless shirts, although, I still couldn't bring myself to wear a sleeveless shirt in public.

We were becoming more grounded in our religious beliefs and had even attended the membership class at church. Although, I still hadn't made too many new friends in our new congregation because I was terrified of being hurt once more by church people. We had met one couple, however, who came out of a UPC church as well. She was so very sweet to me and kind of took me under her wing. While she was mentoring me, she sent me a video of a message about God's grace.

While I knew our initial salvation came to us upon belief, I didn't fully understand how deep God's love and grace was toward his people. Being UPC, I had unintentionally neglected the importance of the cross and significance that selfless act had upon my life.

I became practically addicted to this message. I had never heard anything like it before. It was like once again, a weight had been lifted off of my shoulders and I could breathe in and out completely.

In this message, the minister stated how much emphasis Paul had put upon grace in his epistles to the New Testament churches. At that time, Christians who had been converted from Judaism were trying to enforce their old Jewish laws upon new Gentile Christians. Paul uses the powerfully worded phrase in Galatians chapter three, "Who has bewitched you?" Wow, those are such strong words!

I wanted so badly to share this revelation with my family and old friends! But, if people are not in the place to listen, your words land on deaf ears. I remember feeling the urge to stand on a rooftop with a megaphone and shout, "Nothing you can do will make you righteous before God! Jesus already did that for you on your behalf!"

I knew all too well the feeling of being trapped on the hamster wheel of salvation by works. Feeling not good enough, but trying to follow all the rules to a T just to attempt to be righteous, but falling short again and again. The Bible itself says that those who rely on works of the law are under a curse. (Galatians 3:10) It truly did feel like a curse having to run that race. I wanted others to have the same freedoms I had, and for the first time in my life, I even began questioning the salvation of those who had "fallen from grace" (Galatians 5:4) If the Bible says they are cursed and have fallen from grace, what hope is it for them to have eternal salvation? I also felt strongly convicted that I had allowed myself to be sucked into that legalistic religious system without really ever acknowledging the sacrifice of the cross.

Once again the verse, Galatians 2:21 kept coming to mind:

21. I do not nullify the grace of God, for if righteousness were through the law, then Christ died for no purpose. (ESV)

Yikes, if that isn't heart wrenching? I didn't want Christ to feel like I put him second place to my works. It was by His grace and sacrifice alone I was saved! Nothing I did or could do!

I shared this with my mom, I wanted to see her live her life free from the condemnation she was so conditioned to living under. I think she listened to it, but even though she was becoming increasingly miserable at church, she was not in the place to hear the message. She wasn't at the place in her life to really get it. This made me sad, but I also understood her position. It just seems too good to be true.

Not that I had never heard the story of Jesus on the cross growing up UPC, because I had heard it, but it always seemed to be a bit brushed over; a blip in the church's history trailing behind the Azusa Street Revival and Acts chapter two. Such emphasis was put upon new converts speaking in tongues, the believing in the cross part wasn't even spoken about. It always just seemed like a fairy tale story to me. I had honestly never really sat and thought, "Do I actually believe a man who was all God and at the same time, all man came down from heaven, was born of a virgin, hung on a cross, died, and rose again? And furthermore, by his death,

I am now free from the burden of my despicable sin?" That truly is like a fairy tale. When you stop to think about it, it is pretty unbelievable.

It all began to fall into place for me, and it was at this moment I feel like I was truly saved. I sat and thought, "Do I really believe this? Can I buy into such a miraculous event?" I did, and once again was changed for life.

Now, instead of doing good things to prove to myself, and hopefully God, I was a good person and worthy of His love, I wanted to be a better person simply because I was deeply appreciative of how much love it would take for Jesus Christ to die for me. I wanted to spread genuine love to others because that is what God did for me! It was such a huge paradigm shift in my thinking. Instead of continually believing I was never good enough, I began placing my trust in how God feels about me. John 3:16 and 17, verses I never truly understood before, became beautiful to me.

16. For God so loved the world, that he gave his only Son, that whosoever believes in him should not perish, but have eternal life.

17. For God did not send his Son into the world to condemn the world, but in order that the world might be saved through him. (ESV)

Wow! So refreshing! Let's be honest, I always kind of rolled my eyes to this passage before because it was emphasized in those other churches that didn't have the "truth". But, now the full weight of what those verses are saying was becoming very real.

Our new church also was very much about community service and loving your neighbor. I had never been in a church so dedicated to helping others without a hidden agenda. They did it out of sincere love, and not to trick people into coming to their church building. This was so refreshing to me as well! Love, what a novel concept! (Insert hand to head slap).

One day when I was driving home from a side hustle I had been working for extra cash, I decided I was going to get a tattoo to remind me forever about how I felt in this exact place in my life. I never wanted to take for granted God's grace again. I walked into the tattoo shop and had the verse reference Gal. 2:21 tattooed on my wrist with a small leaf, a replica of the necklace Jereme bought for me. I loved it. A forever reminder of the new life experiencing God's grace and freedoms we were blessed enough to be enjoying.

Chapter 8

Moving On

When we returned from our summer vacation that year, I found out I did get the job at the optometrist office. I was thrilled to be able to accept the position and wear the scrub pants required. Something so small, but before we left the UPC, I would have had to request permission from my boss to wear a scrub skirt. Yes, those look as stupid as they sound. Life seemed to finally be moving on for us.

My heart was still breaking for all of my former friends left in the UPC, but I was coming to the stage of grief of acceptance. It was their choice to be there. If they wanted out badly enough, they could study as I did. The worst part of it all, however, was my mom. My stepdad was still very much active in the church and seemed to agree with everything wholeheartedly. My mom, on the other hand, was depressed and I was told she only sat on the back row and didn't talk to anyone. I knew people had said things to her, to this day, I still don't know all that was said. I was still trying to give them the benefit of the doubt, they were just reacting in the way they thought was best, I felt responsible for my mom's misery. If we had just stayed there, things would still be the same as before.

Around this time, I attended a couple of funerals at my old church. It seemed the most respectable thing to do for the deceased, but this was my first time back in the building since we had left. Feeling guilty about putting my mother through her current situation, I had briefly entertained the idea of visiting there from time to time just so I could sit with her. Those funeral services changed my mind.

Trying to decide what I would wear to the services was a feat in itself. I had thrown out pretty much all of my UPC church attire by this time and even the thought of putting on a knee-length skirt made my skin crawl. I didn't want to be disrespectful, however, so I did end up wearing a dress, but I made sure it was in some way not adhering to their standards. I think for one funeral my slit was higher than my knee and I put on a necklace, and for the other, my dress was a couple of inches above my knee cap.

The first funeral I attended, in the middle of the funeral message, the minister mentioned how he was wealthy and the deceased was not. Really, who says that? During the other message the same minister proceeded to tell the congregation if they ever wanted to see their loved one again, they needed to attend their church. Then in both instances, he promptly went into a message about the UPC's version of the salvation plan. The entire thing was completely inappropriate and unprofessional. I just cringed listening to it. If I had heard those messages while we were still attending that church, it would have bothered me, but somehow I would have pushed it to the back of my mind and justified the behavior in some way. It was a nice break for me that I no longer felt I had to justify anything and I could look at it for what it was, inappropriate.

Oh, and one more thing I forgot to mention, I was asked to sing! One of the people who had passed away had a long history with our family and they had asked me to sing with the ensemble I had sung with for ten years, this group of course as fate would have it, included Barb. The whole experience was so incredibly uncomfortable. She was friendly to me in front of everyone and even asked me if I could get her a discount on glasses at the eye doctor's office I worked for. After the funeral was over, I made a point to approach her and hug her when no one else was around. I sincerely wanted peace between us. I felt like my attempt at reconciling was received a bit coldly as she barely even acknowledged me when I told her I missed her.

Afterward, at both funerals, the people who didn't avoid me completely came up to me and said things both innocent and condescending. One lady told me it was "time to come home and stop this rebellion". It was all I could do to keep my facial expressions from giving away exactly what I was thinking. Anyone who knows me at all knows that this was quite the challenge; most of the time everyone around me knows exactly what is in my head without me having to say a word!

Both funeral experiences sealed it for me. No way could I visit services there and feel comfortable ever again. Too much had transpired. Too much had been said.

After that summer ended and fall had begun, Jordin was invited by our neighbors to go to the church's Halloween trunk or treat. An event they host every year at the end of October, (but never on October 31st because that would be acknowledging Satan's holiday). He was adamant he wanted to go. I allowed him thinking, what harm could come of him getting some candy? Once again, my child came home from one of their events in tears. According to Jordin, a group of

95

teen girls, the same group that had been giving Jocelynn trouble, refused to give him any candy. I mean, seriously? Why was this okay? Were there not any adults supervising that witnessed this? I was furious.

Let me just say right here, at this point, we had been gone a year and a half and I still wanted to try and maintain civil relationships with people. But it felt like every attempt our family had made to keep friendships had failed epically. It was beginning to dawn on me, the only way to move forward past the pain was to completely cut everyone from our past out of our lives and focus on new, healthy relationships looking toward our future. I struggled with the idea of this because I am a Christian, and in being a Christian, I want to be like Christ. I wanted to be strong enough to show them that I still loved them and also to convince them I was indeed still a good person. I didn't want to prove their theories about backsliders correct. Those in the UPC tend to think people who have left feel conviction upon talking to them or going to services and this is why the rebellious don't come around. That could not be farther from the truth. The real reason is, the church member's words and actions, simply make coming around them too painful.

The straw that broke the camel's back for me with Barb was when Barb and mine's mutual friend who had been considering leaving, told me that Barb was complaining to her how I never liked or commented on her social media posts. I felt like I was in middle school again. She knew good and well that would get back to me. That was it. I couldn't deal with the pettiness any more, it was so stupid. I went through my social media friends and cut my list in half. I blocked her number from my phone and private messages. I was officially moving on, and it felt good.

To symbolize putting my past behind me I decided to dye my hair. It sounds so silly now how much anxiety I had about doing something so simple. Some people I know in the UPC do dye their hair, but I am pretty sure it is officially tabooed. Not to mention, dying your hair is damaging and you aren't supposed to be trimming that damage off, so, it seemed stupid to me to damage your hair with no way to fix it. I was experiencing new freedoms all the time and this was one of them. I was so nervous I brought some new-found friends along for support. I almost threw up from the anxiety! Thank goodness I have a great hairstylist, she is always very patient with me! I dyed it auburn and it turned out gorgeous! I loved it! Afterward, we all went out for wine and cheesecake. I felt a wave of independence wash over me once more.

Months went by and I felt like my life was finally starting to come together. I wasn't feeling as lonely as before. I was trying to let some new people into my life, and while I didn't trust them completely, I did allow myself to start making new friends. My kids were becoming involved in the youth activities at church and they seemed to be moving forward as well. I felt myself start to relax and to heal. The thing that seemed to hold me back the most was my parents.

While my biological father was happy to see me leave the church, my mom and my stepdad were still stuck there, along with my stepbrother and his family. I hated the thought of my mom sitting by herself on the back pew during church services and I watched helplessly as she became more and more isolated. I prayed endlessly for her freedom and for somehow God to reveal His grace to them like never before. On several occasions, we had discussed the origins of the UPC and how their beliefs were unfounded and my mom was beginning to understand more and more why we left. Supporting our new found beliefs was the way she saw we were treated when we left. I think my mom felt ashamed and betrayed by the organization she had held dear to her for so long. Slowly my parents started to withdraw from the church and eventually stopped attending altogether. This was a huge burden lifted off my shoulders because I just couldn't bear the thought of my parents living under such bondage. Eventually, my stepbrother moved to a different church, and while it is still a part of the organization, all the ties I had to our old congregation are no longer. It was a relief, to say the least.

I felt like healing was taking place, I felt like my body and soul could be freed from the burdens of trying to live with oppression, then the guilt, and loneliness that followed. We had a huge party at our house to celebrate the new friendships we had made. It was a giant success and it was amazing to get everyone who was helping us move on in one place to mingle and have a good time. My heart was so full of thankfulness and love. I had made it, I had successfully made the transition from religious slave to God's chosen. Life was good!

Chapter 9

One Step Forward Two Steps Back

Not long after our celebratory party, my sense of security in our new life came crashing down. One day while I was mindlessly doing my job at work, I glanced at the doctor's schedule for the day and my heart stopped. A name from my past life popped out at me and I felt like I had been punched in the gut. I was with a patient at the time and it was all I could do to get up calmly and walk to the front office. I lost control, the second panic attack I ever had in my life took over my entire body. My boss was amazing and realized immediately what was going on as I had confided in her before some things about my past. I walked out the back door, collapsed, and started hyperventilating and ugly crying right there in the parking lot. It was then that it dawned on me, I had not moved on as well as I thought I had. My body responded to seeing a name on a computer screen in a way I could not control.

I began having difficulties sleeping and eating. My stomach felt like it was in knots continually. After having a panic attack at work, I was always worried about running into someone in public, what if I had a panic attack again? I started realizing certain words were triggers for me. Words like, "truth" and "holiness" made my skin crawl.

I knew I needed some professional help when I was in choir practice at church one night. The choir was something that I signed up for a year before to meet new people. The director was introducing a document for everyone to sign that went over things such as attendance and stage attire. To be fair, the stipulations were in place to keep a level of professionalism on the platform in front of the whole church, but for me it was personal. We were required to sign documents like these in my old church vowing to pay no less than ten percent of our income to the church and dress in UPC standards at all times, particularly on the platform. There were also silly additional rules like on the platform women had to wear pantyhose, sleeves were to be down to your elbows, and men had to wear ties, things like this.

Once again, I was triggered. Logically, I can understand why a church, especially one as large as ours, would need to have rules in place about clothing. It just looks more professional. However, for me, I could not bring myself to sign a document that stated such things. It felt like I was signing on the dotted line permitting someone else to judge what I was wearing, and that was a huge step backward for me. I was coming to a place in my life of making my own decisions about my clothing choices and I just couldn't do it. I could not allow someone else to make the rules for me in that aspect of my life again, I just couldn't. I ran out of there and drove home as fast as I could.

Defeated, I ended up dropping out of the choir. I was disappointed in myself I couldn't sign a stupid piece of paper, but it was such a physical reaction, I simply could not do it.

To make matters worse, our house had been on the market for a year, and the only offers we had gotten were less than what we paid for the stupid thing years before! I didn't understand it, our realtor couldn't understand it. It was just the market in our area I suppose. But I felt stuck. I thought by physically moving, that would be the epitome of closure. We would be able to start from scratch in a place where our neighbors weren't praying for us to move. I felt as if God was punishing me for something or trying to teach me a very cruel lesson. Every time I walked out of my house I felt judged. My neighbors were nice to our faces, but I knew what they were thinking. We had gotten past our spat as adults should, but the scars still very much remained.

I think until this point, I had been downplaying the amount of emotional and mental stress I had been under. It wasn't until I was at work training someone to take a scan of the inside of my eye that it truly hit me. The doctor in the office took a look at the image and said, "Are you stressed? Your eye has a slight hemorrhage."

Once I started really thinking about it, I realized why I was having such difficulties. I had uprooted my family from an organization that I had completely trusted, lost every friend I ever knew (except for Marie), entertained the thought of possibly having a reprobate mind and going to hell, reinvented my self in a new atmosphere, with new hair, new clothes, and a new job. Life had been quite a roller coaster. I called a doctor.

I didn't have a primary physician at that time so I asked around for recommendations and made an appointment with one. I know that lady thought I was level ten crazy by the end of my appointment, but she was amazing. I looked at her and said, "You don't know me, but I swear I am not a

101

drug addict, I just really need some Xanax!" She, of course, asked me why, and as I told her a little bit of my story, she ever so kindly said, "Honey, you have survived a cult, you're going to need something stronger than Xanax, and a therapist." I love this woman.

She was right, I needed therapy. I had also tossed around the idea the UPC is indeed a cult, and while I am choosing not to get into the specifics here, personally I am convinced it is. But, that is another discussion for another day.

As much as I hate to admit it, the medication helped tremendously. I started sleeping better and was finding I had fewer triggers. I also started writing a blog.

Do you know what the weird thing about that is? People were actually reading it! It began as personal therapy, but I was getting visitors to my site, I quickly realized it could be helping other people as well as myself. I write about my feelings, good or bad, and all the new experiences since leaving legalism. It was and is very therapeutic to get my feelings out of my head and into tangible words. It has also put me in touch with many people from around the globe who have had an experience similar to mine. The fact I am not alone in my quest for religious freedom is reassuring in itself.

The fall I started my blog, Jereme and I were about to leave on a vacation for some much needed time away just the two of us. We planned to hang by the resort pool all week and just veg. I wanted to look good for him, as all wives do for their husbands, so I asked him if he wanted me to wear anything specific. He requested a red bikini.

Dear God! I had never worn a bikini before! I was entirely unsure about how I felt about it. The idea that a woman showing too much skin could cause a man to lust after her thus making him sin was on my mind. What if someone looked at me and I caused him to sin? Would that in itself be a sin? I already had a hard enough time wearing

102

a sleeveless shirt out of my home in fear someone would see. What if someone at some point saw a picture of me in a bikini? Or worse, what if, for some crazy reason, we ran into someone we knew at the pool on vacation? Those kinds of things always seem to happen to me!

As with every other decision I make, I was overthinking it and driving myself insane. I had a conversation about it with a friend who had not been raised in the UPC and I told her all my fears. She just looked at me blankly and said, "It's just a swimsuit!" Huh, why yes it was. It suddenly hit me like a ton of bricks! Yep, no one else on the planet makes themselves crazy over a swimsuit. What do normal people do? They walk into a store, find one they like and buy it, not thinking a thing about it.

So I did. I found a red one online, and bought the stupid thing! Let's be real, I bought high waisted, full coverage bottoms, but hey, it was a bikini none the less! I rocked it! Mom bod and all! And the best part? I didn't even feel a shred of guilt! After my friend so nonchalantly calmed my fears, I came to the realization, it is not my job, nor my business to try and police someone else's mind. So what if some creepy, pervert can't keep his mind out of the gutter? Is that my fault? No! Someone could get just as turned on by seeing me in a parka as in a swimsuit. While men are visual creatures by nature, that does not give them a pass at perverted behavior. I can and should be comfortable being me, and pleasing my husband is my top priority. I had the epiphany that if I didn't dress to please him, someone else may. Would it be that woman's fault? Hell no! It would be on Jereme if he was swayed by another woman. But the least I could do to help my husband was dress in a way that would turn him on!

We had an amazing vacation! I got to spend lots of time lying at the pool in my red bikini looking up from my drink and book in time to see Jereme eyeing me from his chair. It felt so good to know I was attractive to him that I didn't even think about the rest of the people there. My husband thought I was sexy, and that was all that mattered in my world.

After the slight fiasco with the bikini, it seemed things were improving for me. I felt like I had a new outlook. Which seems so silly to say after simply buying a swimsuit, but I was slowly letting go of all of the indoctrination I had received my entire life. It was a turning point for me. I was free of the condemnation I always felt by being me. I was allowing myself to be creative and choose the image I wanted to portray to others. It felt great leaving the house in confidence that whatever I was wearing, whether it was yoga pants and a hoody, or a sleeveless dress it was what I felt like wearing that day. Not clothing that was dictated to me by a church organization.

As year three of our transition was coming to a close, Jereme and I both thought we were in a good place with our past. Yes, we had lost many "friends" along the way, but we were creating new, healthier friendships, the kids included. We got complacent and comfortable. I feel we let our guard down, and because of that, my child suffered.

Jordin decided he wanted to have a sleepover for his birthday and invite some of his newer close friends from church along with our neighbor's son. I should have seen the train wreck coming a mile away.

Things were seemingly moving along smoothly the first hour or so. As smoothly as a twelve-year-old boy sleepover can at least. All of the boys are good kids, and they were all getting along well. Jereme and I were sitting on the couch watching TV when Jordin came out into the living room with my neighbor's son whispering to him. Jordin said, "Mom, he has to tell you something." Immediately I thought, "Oh brother, here it goes!"

This child stood in front of me and said, "My dad told me to be texting him tonight everything that was said to make sure the other boys don't say anything inappropriate. One of them said the girl on the video game has (whispering now) big boobies. I don't want to have to text him that because if he thinks anything is inappropriate I have to go home immediately, and I don't want to do that to Jordin."

I was angry. I felt violated like my neighbor was using his son to spy on us. I just looked at him and said, "Well, I suppose if you think the word boob is inappropriate, go ask them nicely not to say it anymore. As far as texting your dad is concerned, that is between you and him, I am not going to tell you what to do about that."

He went downstairs with the rest of the boys and things were quiet for about twenty minutes or so, then Jordin came up the stairs crying. I took him to the other room and asked him what in the world was going on. He proceeded to tell me, the neighbor's child told him he had heard the other boys saying "the F-word and the N-word". Now I was beyond mad, I was absolutely irate. I looked at Jordin and said, "Did you hear them say those things, or did he say that he heard them?" Jordin said he hadn't personally heard the boys say anything like that.

I walked into the room where the boy from next door was gathering his things. All of the other boys were in there and I asked all of them collectively what, if anything, was said that was inappropriate. They all looked at me blankly and one boy said, "Well, I hit my elbow and I said son of a gun. Then I was watching a video on my phone and I didn't know the 'H' word was in it, but when I heard it, I immediately turned it off because I didn't want him (neighbor kid) to get offended." The neighbor's child didn't refute any of this. The realization hit me then and there; he was lying. Perhaps because he felt pressured by his father to find something that could be deemed offensive and send him straight home, I am really not for certain. I was so heartbroken for Jordin. His best friend had completely betrayed him.

There were several things wrong with this picture. Number one, all of the boys that were at my home that evening are good, Christian boys from strong families. It's not like they were smoking pot in my basement or anything. Number two, Jordin had planned this sleepover for weeks around my neighbor's strict beliefs. He sincerely didn't want anything to offend his friend. He planned a G rated movie, warned his other friends ahead of time not to be too rambunctious, and made sure to tell them not to watch any "offensive" YouTube videos. Number three, one of the children at the sleepover was mixed race. We are from a very Caucasian area and maybe this was a novelty for my neighbor's child who attended a tiny private school and lived a small, sheltered life, but this was the child he was blaming everything on. This is the point that made Jordin just livid. When it all came out in the end, I found out the neighbor's son was the one that was saying the 'N' word thinking it was funny. When Jordin told him that wasn't cool, that is when he said he had heard the other kid say it. I find it unbelievable that there were a total of eight people in that room, and he was the only one who heard that kid say anything "inappropriate".

Not long after my neighbor's boy left, Jordin came bounding up the steps with a huge smile on his face. "Mom, we are actually having a better time now that we can be more relaxed and not worry about every little thing offending him!" I was happy for him but crushed on the inside at the same time. I knew their friendship would never be the same.

Now, if my child had been at a sleepover and had called to tell me inappropriate things were going on, the first thing I would do would be to call the other child's parents to see what was happening. Maybe that is just me, but to this day, my neighbors have never said a word. In fact, pretty much the opposite thing happened. Two days after the party, my neighbor posted a nice, long post on Facebook including a picture of his son and how much of a good, Godly child he was. I wanted to vomit.

I could just imagine what had happened. His father had warned him about all the inappropriate things the "worldly boys" from the non-denominational church would be doing at this party. Set him up as a spy essentially to get the scoop on everything us backsliders were doing in our own home. When nothing significant happened, that child felt so much pressure from his father he made something up. I feel like he chose the child who looked different than him as a scapegoat because, to be honest, many UPC people around this area can come across pretty racist. I don't think that child himself is a bigot, but I feel like that is the overall vibe in his environment. But, I am just speculating, since I don't know their actual reasons for doing what they did. I probably don't want to anyway. Regardless of the reason, the entire situation was tragic.

Jordin struggled with what to do with this situation for weeks. He wanted to remain friends with our neighbor's son, but he felt like what he did was so despicably wrong, he felt he simply could not be friends with someone who would lie and treat his other friends the way he had. I didn't want to tell him what to do at all; it had to be his decision alone. He did notice however that it was much less stressful for him to not have to walk on eggshells all the time to not offend the neighbors. I can honestly say, he prayed and earnestly sought what the Lord would want him to do. In the end, he decided he could not remain such close friends with someone who would treat others in that manner. I was super proud of him for his dignity and courage to set healthy boundaries, but heartbroken he had to give up a lifetime of friendship because of ignorance.

He told the neighbor's son he would still be cordial to him and wasn't going to stay mad at him, he had forgiven him, but at the same time felt like their season of friendship was over. The other child called him stupid and said he hated him and huffed off. His behavior just proved to Jordin he ultimately did the right thing. The next day the child's father was outside ten feet from where Jordin and I were standing. I greeted him in an effort to maintain some level of peace. He blatantly ignored both of us. Jordin just looked up at me with sad eyes. My heart sank.

I decided that week I would be officially finished with all people and things related to the UPC. For three years by this point, I tried my best to preserve a friendly environment with our neighbors. After this incident, I was done. It took way more effort on my part to try and not step on their toes, it just wasn't worth the stress to me. I finally let go of any hope of reconciling our friendship, and a huge weight was lifted from my shoulders. As much as I want to represent the love of God in my daily life, I have learned sometimes you can forgive people, but protect yourself and your family by loving them from a distance. I have made peace with it. We are still friendly, but not the friends we once were.

Chapter 10

Current Situation

As I said from the beginning, I don't have all of my ducks in a row. As the saying goes, I have squirrels and they are running everywhere! I am still in the process of learning and growing. I am finding new things out about myself every day. I don't pretend to have all of the answers, but I do claim to be actively searching for them.

As I have allowed myself to slowly let go of the past, it has helped me begin to heal. After being diagnosed with PTSD, I started seeing a therapist who specializes in spiritual abuse. My visits with her seem to be helping bring some peace.

After a few years in our current church, we finally decided to let our walls down and join a small group. They push these small groups of people meeting in other's homes as a way to make friends and support one another in prayer and life. Friendships have been created and bonds are starting to grow. I am encouraged my heart feels free enough again to be open to the possibility of allowing people in my life.

The kids are doing fantastic and thriving in our current church situation. I have noticed that when things do come up that are questionable for their wellbeing, I have the voice to speak up. This ability is something I never possessed before, and I am ashamed to say, I let others abuse that situation at my children's expense.

I am still working on my relationship with my biological father. Both of us have lots of scars we need to sort through. I refuse to give up because that is just not who I am. Family is important. I have noticed, however, since leaving the UPC, I now possess the capability to create healthy boundaries between him and me. Boundaries sound counterproductive, but they give us both the space we need to heal.

Since leaving the UPC, I have had several others reach out to me with questions or stories about their time in the organization. My blog has been a resource to connect with others from around the world. It seems to me; my experiences while inside the church and leaving are not unique. This is an epidemic. It makes me sad and angry that lifetimes of friendships have been lost over doctrinal differences. Every one of them have a story. Not one person I know has left this organization unscathed.

This book is not to bash the UPC in any way, nor is that my intention with my blog. Clearly, those whom I encountered on my journey don't necessarily represent an entire organization. However, my experience is eerily similar to many, many others I have discovered since speaking out. Coincidence? Maybe. But maybe there is more to it than that. When so many people leaving have similar stories about rejection, judgment, and hate, common sense tells me there is a theme. The question then comes to mind, why? Why do UPC people tend to respond to those leaving in this manner? I reacted the same way to people leaving when I was in the organization, the attitude is rampant.

A common belief among the UPC is that people leave out of rebellion. This, at least in my case, could not be further from the truth. The organization's belief system makes it nearly impossible for those who have stayed to look at ex-members as friends. This idea truly creates an us versus them mentality.

The true tragedy of this reality is many good people are honestly doing the very best they know how, but are tangled up in this religion. Many people I know are living a life of spiritual bondage with the purest intentions. They feel oppressed, but don't know why. They are questioning things that maybe don't feel right to them, dismissing it as their issue. Wanting to ask questions or even leave, but can't because they fear losing relationships with loved ones or worse, having a reprobate mind and going to hell. This is why I cannot keep my mouth shut. They are the reason why I want to share my story.

When the revelation of God's unconditional love and grace was first brought to light in my life, I just wanted to stand on the rooftops and shout it to the world. I wanted to tell the people living a life of bondage, you don't have to live this way! This book is closing a chapter for me. I am writing to symbolize I have moved on and have grown from the past, but it is so much more. It is my way of shouting from the rooftops to those stuck in the routine of religious tradition and legalism that God wants to set them free. After all, Jesus did say, His yoke is easy and his burden is light.

I had dinner with a group of old friends the other day, people who were raised in a variety of religions. The common theme among us was church hurt. It is a very real thing that can scar people for a lifetime. All Christians have experienced it to varying degrees in one way or another.

111

While my personal experience is with the UPC, legalism, judgementalism, racism, and shunning occurs quite commonly among religious groups whether we would like to admit it to ourselves or not. I often find myself asking, how many people have we lost to Christianity because of our lack of love or empathy? My heart bleeds not only for those who have walked away from God altogether because of spiritual abuse but also for those who are still in the bondage of a religious system. Living for God is not about what church you belong to, but about love.

James 1:27 says this in the ESV:

27. Religion that is pure and undefiled before God the Father is this: to visit orphans and widows in their affliction, and to keep oneself unstained from the world.

My intention is not to bring negativity to a denomination, but to shine a light on the beautifully freeing gift of God's grace. There is such a wave of oppression among the UPC, women especially. I can see the despair and hopelessness in their eyes as I pass by them on the street. I know the pain, I have lived it. The pain of never being good enough, ashamed of your own body and curves, the feeling of never being happy with your appearance, and never being able to express yourself because you are constantly having to conform to the regulations of your religion.

The people who wronged me while leaving were only responding in the way they were taught. They honestly feared for my soul and were made to believe by their religion that by ignoring me, gaslighting me, and trying to manipulate my other friends to walk away from me they were doing me an eternal favor. They are so afraid of their God; they honestly think this is how He behaves and would approve of their tactics.

112

While I am far from perfect, far from finished processing all of the layers of trauma that come from spiritual abuse, I am happy. I am deep down sure of my salvation, and daily in awe of the love and mercy that Jesus bestowed upon me. I am no better than anyone in the United Pentecostal Church, I am no better than the Catholic, the agnostic, the atheist. The fact of the matter is, Christ died for our sins no matter what our beliefs. He knew ahead of time that not all would accept his free gift of salvation and yet He did it anyway. That is pure love.

Jesus said the first and most important commandment is love. Love God and love your neighbor, it is that simple. Loving your neighbor does not mean you agree with everything they do, but as Peter said in 1 Peter 3:15; defend your faith with gentleness and respect. If the constituents of the UPC would acknowledge those two Biblical theologies in their tactics, I wouldn't even be writing this right now. If those who left felt love with gentleness and respect the organization would not be considered by many to be a cult.

Mike Rinder, a former Scientologist, said this after leaving his religion:

"The difference between a religion and a cult is what happens when you try to leave."

Let that sink in a moment. The UPC doesn't publically teach the practice of shunning, but they have certainly mastered the craft of it. Truth be told, I feel like they are afraid. They can see the happiness in the eyes of those who have left and it scares them. They are so conditioned to see the bad in the world, that anything beyond the tiny bubble of their sanctuary is terrifying.

But I am here to say, there is life after the UPC! You can be a follower of Christ, as a woman who wears pants. If you cut your hair, you don't lose some sort of angelic power. If you have on makeup, you aren't a whore and you can still raise your hands to worship your Savior. There is hope after leaving! You don't have to live every moment of your life hiding behind a fake smile and lifeless eyes! You can have a positive body image and live for God. There are people in the world that you can have healthy friendships with who aren't going to leave you high and dry if you disagree with them.

If you find you are wanting to leave, questioning things, or have left the UPC and are needing resources there are support groups on Facebook, books, and blogs written by people who have already been there. There are people who have made it and are now living a life free in Jesus. Find someone to confide in, get a therapist if necessary. It really is possible to be happy and live for God at the same time! Follow what your heart is telling you, maybe it isn't you that is making you so miserable, maybe it is God trying to lead you out of bondage and into his freedom. Listen to his still, small voice telling you something is amiss.

As insurmountable as leaving seems at the moment, bigger better things are possible I promise. Good luck in finding your freedom in Jesus!

Resources and Relevant Scriptures

Fudge, Thomas A., *Christianity Without the Cross: A history of Salvation in Oneness Pentecostalism.* Universal Publishers,
2003.

Lewis, Daniel J., *Journey Out: of the United Pentecostal Church.* Amazon Kindle,
2015

December, 1945. *Our Paper*. Pentecostal Harold. Page 6.
http://www.1stapostolic.org/oldpublications.html

Spiritualabuse.org

http://www.dividetheword.blog

http://www.findingmyfreedomdoingmylife.wordpress.com

Yadon, Loren, *Tragedy of War.* Landmark Conference. 1993. YouTube.
https://www.youtube.com/watch?v=NbE1dhHrZCo

Helpful scriptures concerning salvation:

Mark 16:16
John 3:16-17
Acts 2:21
Acts 16:30-31
Romans 1:16
Romans 2:22-26
Romans 10:9-13
Galatians 2:16
Galatians 3:22
Ephesians 1:13
Ephesians 2:8

Made in the USA
Columbia, SC
18 August 2019